THE DOMESTIC MOSAIC

CANADIAN INSTITUTE OF INTERNATIONAL AFFAIRS

THE DOMESTIC MOSAIC

Domestic Groups and Canadian Foreign Policy

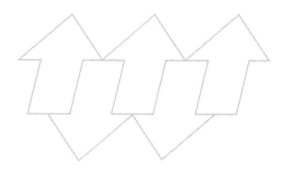

ELIZABETH RIDDELL-DIXON

$7.00 PREPAID

© Canadian Institute of International Affairs 1985
15 King's College Circle
Toronto, Canada M5S 2V9

Canadian Cataloguing in Publication Data

Riddell-Dixon, Elizabeth M. (Elizabeth Mary), 1954–
The domestic mosaic

(Domestic sources of Canadian foreign policy ; 1)
Bibliography: p.
Includes index.
ISBN 0-919084-47-8

1. Pressure groups – Canada.   2. Canada – Foreign
relations – 1945-   I. Canadian Institute of
International Affairs.   II. Title.   III. Series.

JL148.5.R52 1984   322.43'0971   C84-099600-4

50,398

The Institute has as its objects the stimulation in Canada
of a more informed opinion on international affairs
and more particularly on Canada's international relations and
interests, and the study of international affairs in its broadest sense
with primary emphasis on the economic, political, diplomatic, and
defence roles and interests of Canada. The Institute as such
is precluded by its constitution from expressing an opinion
on any aspect of world affairs. The views expressed in this volume
are therefore those of the author.

CONTENTS

v

FOREWORD

The objective of the Canadian Institute of International Affairs is to contribute to a better understanding of Canada's foreign policy. As a voluntary organization with members and branches across the country, the Institute has, since its founding in 1928, brought together interested Canadians from the private sector, academia, and government to discuss and debate issues in international affairs. As a source of informed analysis and commentary, the Institute has a proud record of responsibility for a considerable number of the books and articles which have chronicled the history, analyzed the underlying factors, and assessed the merits of Canada's actions in the world. For example, a pioneering contribution to this record, *Canada Looks Abroad*, by R.A. MacKay and E.B. Rogers, set a high standard for future work and is still a model today, almost half a century after its publication.

From time to time, the CIIA has been able to secure funding for special research projects. In 1981, the generous support of the Donner Canadian Foundation allowed the Institute to establish an in-house research programme on a permanent basis, a major thrust of the first phase of which was the beginning of a systematic and comprehensive examination of the domestic sources of Canada's foreign policies. This focus seems appropriate for the Institute, given its nature and its roots in those domestic sources. But such an examination is needed, regardless of its locus. Most writings on Canada and international affairs are by nature either descriptive or prescriptive. Too few are primarily analytical, or explain the policies being pursued. Too few, in other words, attempt to answer the questions: 'Why? What are the factors at work here?'

This is particularly the case in the realm of domestic societal sources. A good deal is known about the predilections of prime ministers, past and present, and about the workings and views of officialdom in the Department of External Affairs. However, less is known about the factors within the Canadian society, economy, and polity which influence foreign policies, and how such influence is exerted. Beyond a lingering, fairly common – and almost certainly incorrect – assumption that these factors do not matter much, there is little general understanding of the subject. There are few accepted propositions and few, if any, well-recognized analytical models or theories. Perhaps it is the lot of lesser powers that the domestic roots of their foreign policies are more easily ignored. Perhaps the pomp and ceremony of international diplomacy make it difficult for Canadians to recall the admonitions of leaders who have noted that 'foreign policy is domestic politics with its hat on' or that 'foreign policy ... is the extension abroad of national policies.'

Whatever the reason, there is no book or monograph exploring the foreign policy role of the Canadian Parliament and the political pressures to which members of parliament and senators respond. There is no recent broad treatment of the growing and changing involvements of provincial governments in external affairs. There is no major book or monograph analyzing the influence of the media or of public opinion in the making of foreign policy. And, up to now, there has been no comprehensive treatment of interest groups in Canada active in foreign policy issues.

Elizabeth Riddell-Dixon has now provided that treatment. She has undertaken the first broad survey of domestic interest groups, identifying over 200 of them, describing their interests and activities, and discussing their role in decision-making. The groups are broken down into categories depending on the primary basis of affiliation for their members (business, including the resource sectors; agricultural; labour; professions, including educational associations; consumer; veteran/military support; women's; religious; ethnic; citizens; and 'special' foreign policy). *The Domestic Mosaic* offers some general conclusions regarding the groups and their representations on foreign policy issues. The emphasis, however, is on description and classification rather than on theory. Given the diversity of these groups, it is not possible for such a survey to provide an in-depth analysis of the involvement of any group – much less all groups – in the policy process; what it does provide is a unified and invaluable foundation on which subsequent analyses can be based.

This publication is the first in a series of monographs which will explore the domestic sources of Canada's policies abroad. Each volume in the series will examine a particular type of influence arising within the domestic environment. It is the hope of the Institute that this series will make a major contribution to our understanding of foreign policy and international affairs. Support of the series has been provided by an institutional grant to the CIIA from the Donner Canadian Foundation. The commitment of the Foundation to research in this area is long standing and well known, and its support is gratefully acknowledged.

DON MUNTON

PREFACE

In recent years, greater attention has been paid to the role of interest groups and the foreign policy making process in Canada. In recognition of the need to examine this topic further, the Canadian Institute of International Affairs hosted a conference on 'Domestic Groups and Foreign Policy' in Ottawa in June 1982. Participants at the conference included group representatives, federal civil servants, and academics. This monograph began as a project for that conference. It set out to identify a broad range of interest groups involved in a variety of foreign policy issues. The study provided resource information on which government officials, academics, and interest group representatives could draw. Most of the civil servants interviewed knew only about the involvements of groups with which they had direct contact. In addition, their knowledge of the groups' activities was often limited to their particular area of specialization. Similarly, in order to facilitate in-depth studies, academics tend to focus their research fairly narrowly. Without being asked, many of the interest group representatives interviewed said that they would find the study a useful aid in identifying potential allies and opposition and in providing some indication of where their respective groups fit into the overall foreign policy making process.

Several stages were involved in the compilation of this study. In order to identify the relevant interest groups, lists of groups with potential involvement in foreign policy issues were compiled, primarily from directories of Canadian associations. Efforts were then made to contact these groups in person if possible or by telephone and/or mail. Most of the information contained in the survey was drawn from interviews with interest group representatives and with federal civil servants, primarily but not exclusively in the Department of External Affairs. Additional data were gathered from interviews with scholars and knowledgeable third parties, such as the director of the Parliamentary Centre for Foreign Affairs and Foreign Trade. Information also came from printed materials produced by the groups themselves and, to a lesser extent, from academics. Based on the information gathered, an initial draft of the study was compiled and presented to the CIIA's conference on domestic groups and foreign policy. Participants at the conference were invited to comment on the project and several helpful suggestions were made.

Following the conference, relevant sections of the study were sent for comment and suggestions to the groups included. At the same time, additional interviews were conducted and questionnaires were sent to groups which could not be contacted by telephone. Since research for the monograph was completed by December 1982, some of the information, especially that contained in appendix B, may be out of date.

Interviews were chosen as the primary source of information because they were the most efficient means of acquiring data not available in printed form. In addition to supplying information about specific groups, these discussions provided some insights into how the political system works and which groups tend to be most active. Research for the study was greatly facilitated by the willingness of so many interest group representatives to discuss the foreign policy interests and activities of their groups. The federal civil servants who shared information about their interest group contacts were also of enormous help.

The author would like to thank the staff of the Canadian Institute of International Affairs for its assistance in the preparation of this paper. Special thanks are due to Don Munton for his guidance and to Gayle Fraser for her excellent editorial work and invaluable support.

September 1984   E.R-D.

THE DOMESTIC MOSAIC

INTRODUCTION

When Israel invaded Lebanon in the summer of 1982, the Committee of Concerned Canadian Jews sponsored an advertisement in the *Toronto Star* urging Canadians, especially those within the Jewish community, to write to the Israeli ambassador in Ottawa to protest the invasion.[1] One week later, in a demonstration against both the chemical pollution of the Niagara River and the Great Lakes and cutbacks in the United States Environmental Protection Agency, two representatives of Greenpeace attached themselves to a rock cliff 60 feet above the churning Niagara River. When President Zia ul-Haq of Pakistan visited Ottawa in December 1982, three pages of advertisements appeared in the *Toronto Star*.[2] Concerned Pakistani Canadians sponsored an advertisement welcoming the president and pointing out the improvements in Pakistan under his administration.[3] In contrast, the Council of Concerned Pakistanis Abroad was reported to be organizing a protest during the president's visit because of his administration's violation of human rights.[4] These are only a few of many instances one could cite to show that Canadians – politicians, representatives of non-governmental organizations, the media, and members of the general public – are becoming increasingly concerned about international developments and aware of the impact which such developments have on life in Canada.[5]

As interest in foreign affairs grows, so does the potential for a greater divergence of opinions on what Canada's foreign policies should be. However, in spite of the proliferation and growing significance of domestic interest groups, their role in the Canadian foreign policy making process has been, until very recently, a neglected field of study. Research in this area tends to focus on the involvement of an interest group, or a type of interest group, in one particular issue or event. This paper identifies and discusses a wide range of interest groups involved in the foreign policy making process. Its goal is to provide a better understanding of the number and diversity of these groups. It also seeks to highlight the breadth of foreign policy issues and the interrelationship which exists amongst them.

It is perhaps useful to begin with a definition of the terms 'interest group' and 'foreign policy' and with an outline of the methodology chosen. (See appendix A for a note on methodology.) A typology was constructed to facilitate the classification of interest groups involved in the foreign policy making process. Under each category, the survey identifies and provides some information as to the characteristics, foreign policy interests, and activities of as many of the key actors as possible. The names, dates of founding, addresses, telephone numbers, and a contact person for each group are appended, as is similar information for a wider range of groups not discussed in the body of the paper because of time restrictions, inaccessibility, or because they are less actively involved in the foreign policy making process.

The term 'interest group' has been defined differently by various scholars. Frequently distinctions are drawn between 'interest' and 'pressure' groups on the basis of whether or not demands are made to government in support of the group's goals. The strategies, goals, and activities of most groups vary with the issue at stake. Given the pervasiveness of government involvement in so many areas of Canadian society, virtually all interest groups approach the government at some point in support of their goals. The interest groups included in this study do seek access to government decision-makers, although the nature and the level of the contact varies with the issue at stake and the characteristics of the particular group.

For purposes of this study the term 'interest group' refers to '... collectivities organized around an explicit value on behalf of which essentially politi-

4

cal demands are made vis-à-vis government, other groups, and the general public.'[6] This definition conveys the concepts of recognized common interests and articulated demands. The term is qualified further to apply only to a non-profit organization whose primary objective is to represent the common goals of its members. As a result, private firms and educational institutions are not considered interest groups, while business associations, such as the Canadian Business and Industry International Advisory Committee, and organizations representing educational institutions, such as the Association of Canadian Community Colleges, qualify under the definition. Interest groups are independent of government control, although they may receive some public funding for their operational expenses or for specific projects. Members of interest groups may be individuals, institutions, corporations, or associations.

Foreign policy is defined as the decisions adopted and pursued by the official representatives, both political and bureaucratic, of the federal government, in order to influence the behaviour of external actors. Although the provinces are becoming increasingly interested in areas such as trade and aid, foreign policy making is considered only in terms of the federal government. Virtually all interest groups deal only with Ottawa in seeking to influence the formulation or implementation of government foreign policy.

In spite of their numbers and the wide diversity in their characteristics, goals, activities, and resources, interest groups also display certain similarities. In order to facilitate their study, it is both possible and useful, therefore, to classify together groups with common characteristics. The groups discussed here are categorized according to the primary basis of affiliation for their members. In other words, why does a person or an organization join a particular interest group? What is the main characteristic which members share?

An initial distinction is made between economic and non-economic groups.[7] For the former, the primary basis of affiliation is that members share direct economic stakes in the foreign policy making process, which they jointly seek to protect and promote, while the latter pursue goals which are not related directly to the economic well-being of their members. Under the heading of 'economic' there are five subcategories: business, including the resource sectors; agricultural; labour; professional, including educational associations; and consumer. The non-economic classifications include veteran/military

5

support, women's, religious, ethnic, citizens, and special foreign policy.

There are many other factors – size, the issues pursued, the geographic constituency served by the group, and whether the group is institutionalized or ad hoc – which could have been chosen as the basis for categorizing interest groups. Nonetheless, there are several reasons for basing the typology on the primary basis of affiliation. In the first place, it provides some indication of the scope of a group's interests, both domestic and international, and of where its priorities lie. Secondly, it is neutral and conveys no value judgments about the goals of the groups or about their right to participate in the system. Thirdly, since groups within a category, and especially those within a subcategory, are likely to have similar areas of interest, the typology provides an indication of which groups are likely to be involved on a particular issue. Fourthly, by classifying groups according to their primary basis of affiliation, rather than their foreign policy interests, the degree of overlap between categories is minimized. For example, the members of the Friends Service Committee are Quakers whose primary international objective, world peace, stems from religious beliefs. In order to achieve world peace, the Friends promote international development and human rights, as well as disarmament. The Canadian Friends Service Committee is classified as a religious group because the primary basis of affiliation for its members is shared religious beliefs. Although the typology minimizes the degree of overlap between categories, discretion had to be exercised in cases where a group's basis of affiliation qualified it for more than one category.

ECONOMIC GROUPS

BUSINESS

A wide variety of business groups participate in the foreign policy making process. The foreign policy interests of most of these groups revolve around trade and tariff issues, although there is significant divergence of opinions within and among groups. Import associations generally favour trade liberalization while Canadian manufacturers who produce for the domestic market frequently support protectionist measures. Some groups, such as the Textile Trade Association whose members include both importers and manufacturers, try to establish a balance between tariff barriers and freer trade.

Given the significance of government policies for the commercial viability of Canadian companies, business groups, especially the large umbrella organizations, closely monitor developments in Ottawa and most have regular contact with government officers. Some groups, such as the Canadian Trucking Association, have offices and representatives in Ottawa to facilitate these contacts, while the executive officers of other groups, such as the Canadian Association – Latin America and Caribbean, commute to the capital on a regular basis. Still other groups, such as the Canadian Manufacturers' Association, utilize both methods of liaison. Efforts are made to cultivate as many access points as possible at the bureaucratic, ministerial, and parliamentary committee levels. Contacts with departments and committees vary from group to group depending on their overall goals and the specific issues at stake. Business groups tend to approach lower and middle level bureaucrats on the premises that policy becomes more set and less easy to change the higher up it moves and that the lower level bureaucrats rely on business for information and hence there exists, at least to some extent, a reciprocity of dependency. However, business groups also try to maintain contacts at the cabinet level. If business fails to exert influence at the lower levels of the bureaucracy on an important issue, the chief executive officers from relevant major corporations will jointly approach cabinet ministers. Such activities are frequently co-ordinated by the large umbrella associations.

A common complaint among business organizations is that frequent cabinet shuffles and personnel changes within the civil service undermine the development of regular government contacts. The relatively short-term pattern of government planning poses additional problems for industries, such as the aerospace product manufacturers, which require a long lead-time to develop their advanced technology.

Business groups can be subdivided according to their overall orientations. Some associations, such as the Canadian Business and Industry International

Advisory Committee (CBIIAC), are concerned with a wide range of international issues pertaining to business and industry, while others confine their activities to a particular geographic area or to a specific industry or sector of the economy. The groups accorded greatest importance by the civil servants were CBIIAC and its seven member associations. Traditionally these groups have dealt most closely on international matters with the Department of Industry, Trade and Commerce; however, the departmental re-organization in February 1982 placed the trade commissions within the Department of External Affairs and may have made that department the most important contact point. The re-organization not only disrupts former patterns of interaction, but also presents problems for groups involved in exporting products because it separates the trade commissioners from the sector branches, which remain within the Department of Industry, Trade and Commerce. Depending on the interests of a group and the issue under consideration, regular contacts are also maintained with a variety of departments, including the Department of Finance and Revenue Canada in connection with tax treaties, the Department of Labour with regard to Canada's position on labour regulations at the International Labour Organization, and Environment Canada in connection with international industrial standards.

CBIIAC is the umbrella group representing the interests of the Canadian business community in foreign policy areas. It was founded in 1977 to promote co-operation amongst the Canadian business community and to coordinate viewpoints when approaching government. Its members are some of the most active and respected business umbrella groups in Canada: the Canadian Chamber of Commerce, the Canadian Council of the International Chamber of Commerce, the Canadian Manufacturers' Association, the Canadian Association – Latin America and Caribbean, the Canadian Committee of the Pacific Basin Economic Council, the Canadian Export Association, and the Canadian Importers Association. While CBIIAC seeks to protect and promote the interests of Canadian business in a wide variety of foreign trade policies, its concern also extends to environmental safeguards, labour codes, and questions of aid to the Third World. Policies on all these issues are developed in steering committees, each of which is managed by one of CBIIAC's constituent members. The committees also liaise with intergovernmental committees and with international business organizations. In addition to their co-operative work, CBIIAC's members participate independently in the foreign policy making process. There is some overlap in membership among these groups. For example, half of the members of the Canadian Export Association are manufacturing companies which also belong to the Canadian Manufacturers' Association. CBIIAC depends solely on its members for funding.

The largest business association in Canada is the Canadian Chamber of Commerce. It has a voting membership of 650 local chambers of commerce and boards of trade and 125,000 affiliated members representing 5000 corporations. It has offices in five Canadian cities east of Winnipeg and sales representatives across the country. Although it is mainly concerned with domestic issues, the importance of developments outside the country to the commercial operations of Canadian companies is recognized. The Chamber's trade policy objectives tend to focus on the macro level and to fall within one of two categories. The international affairs committee deals with general trade policies, tariffs, and export promotion. Issues pertaining to trade between Canada and particular states, the most important of which are the United States and the United Kingdom, are dealt with in bilateral committees. Most of the organization's funding comes from the business community, although the local chambers of commerce and boards of trade also contribute.

It is important to distinguish here between bona fide chambers of commerce and organizations which use the title but are really promotion offices sponsored by foreign governments. The Canada-Germany, Canada-Netherlands, and Canada-France Chambers of Commerce fall into the latter category. Three of the most prominent bona fide chambers are the Brazil-Canada Chamber of Commerce, the Canada-Japan Trade Council, and the Swiss Canadian Chamber of Commerce, all of which qualify for inclusion in this study.

The Brazil-Canada Chamber of Commerce is a member of the Canadian Chamber of Commerce and has links with the Canadian Council of the International Chamber of Commerce. Its main objective is to foster closer economic relations in the form of trade and investment between Canada and Brazil, although it also encourages cultural ties. Its 60 members include Canadian companies working in, importing from, and exporting to Brazil; Brazil-ian companies operating in Canada; and the governments of Quebec and Alberta. The corporate membership of the Brazil-Canada Chamber of Commerce includes some very large companies, such as Canada's chartered banks and Alcan, as well as some small businesses. Funding for the Brazil-Canada Chamber of Commerce comes from its membership, although it does receive payment for government contract work.

The Canada-Japan Trade Council promotes trade and commercial relations between the two countries. While three-quarters of the Council's 500 members are Canadians, it also has some members in Japan and in the United States. Although the vast majority of its members are corporations, some municipal development commissions, government departments, and individuals also belong. The major objective of the Council is to inform Canadian business people about markets and commercial opportunities in Japan. To this end, it publishes a newsletter and information on specific topics of interest to its members, conducts a major annual study, organizes meetings and symposia across Canada to cater to regional needs, and facilitates the establishment of mutually beneficial business interests. Although the Council avoids direct involvement in business negotiations or in defending its members in law suits, it will act as a mediator upon request.

While the Canada-Japan Trade Council encourages greater liberalization of trade between the two countries, it does not lobby either government for specific policy changes. The council does liaise with government officials and has presented briefs, when invited to do so. A large proportion of the Council's financial support comes from Japan, although it also receives funding from its Canadian members.

The Swiss Canadian Chamber of Commerce promotes business relations between Canada and Switzerland and assists Swiss businesses in Canada and Canadian subsidiaries in Switzerland in their commercial operations. There are two separate sections in Canada, one in Toronto and one in Montreal. The former's 250 members and the latter's 400 members include most of the major European and Canadian banks, airlines, and manufacturing companies, as well as business and professional people from both countries. The work of the Swiss Canadian Chamber of Commerce, including the publication of its bulletin, is financed by its membership.

While there is some overlap in staff and membership between the Canadian Chamber of Commerce and the Canadian Council of the International Chamber of Commerce, the two organizations are independent. As the former's primary focus is national and the latter's is international, they tend to pursue separate policy objectives. The major Canadian banks and certain large corporations, such as Alcan, belong to both organizations. However, the membership of the Canadian Chamber tends to be composed of small and medium sized firms, while the members of the International Chamber are primarily large companies with broad worldwide interests. The Canadian Council of the International Chamber of Commerce promotes trade and business ties between Canada and other countries, monitors developments in the international environment which affect Canada's foreign trade and commerce, encourages co-operation among a wide range of business organizations within Canada and among these organizations and similar groups abroad, represents the interests of it members at the International Chamber of Commerce in Paris, and promotes global peace. Like the Canadian Chamber of Commerce, it is funded by the Canadian business community.

The Canadian Importers Association represents approximately 840 firms which have a direct or indirect interest in Canada's international trade. The Association's principal foreign policy goal is the reduction of tariff and non-tariff barriers, although it is also concerned with improving Canada's trading position generally. In pursuing its foreign policy objectives, it is in frequent contact with the federal government, especially with Revenue Canada concerning administrative, customs, and tax issues, with the Department of Finance regarding import policies, and with the divisions formerly in the Department of Industry, Trade and Commerce that are now located in the Department of External Affairs. In addition to pursuing its policy objectives, the Association informs its members of developments relevant to their commercial operations through regular publications and through seminars, conferences, and briefs. The Association relies entirely on its membership for funding. Its foreign policy objectives are shared by other organizations, such as the Retail Council of Canada and the Retail Merchants Association of Canada, both of which represent Canadian merchants who would benefit from importing goods more cheaply.

The Canadian Export Association represents all of Canada's 500 export corporations. Its membership is divided evenly between manufacturers and firms in related service sectors such as banking and transportation. The Association advocates policies which would create an environment conducive to increased exports. Its foreign policy objectives focus on greater trade liberalization, in order to increase access to foreign markets, and government assistance to exporters, by way of competitive export financing and better tax concessions for Canadians employed abroad on export projects. In order to keep its membership informed of developments in Canada and abroad, the Canadian Export Association publishes three monthly newsletters: *Export News, Export Digest,* and *Export USA.* The Association relies solely on its membership for its financial resources.

The Canadian Manufacturers' Association (CMA) represents over 80 per cent of the manufacturing potential in Canada. Its primary concern is the development of favourable domestic policies, including those related to taxation, labour relations, and the maintenance of a flexible business atmosphere conducive to investment. As international affairs affect the economic environment within Canada, the importance of foreign policy is recognized. The major foreign policy goal of the CMA is the promotion of international trade, with particular emphasis on Canadian exports. Consequently, the CMA supports greater trade liberalization, especially the reduction of barriers to Canadian exports. Given its size and the areas of activity of its members, the Canadian Manufacturers' Association tends to deal more with questions of macro- rather than micro-economic policy. In support of its objectives, the Association maintains regular contacts with the federal government.

Membership in the CMA ranges from 8300 to 8500 and is open to any manufacturing company which has more than five employees. Although the CMA's membership includes some large companies, such as Alcan, 75 per cent of its members have less than 100 employees. While these small companies have great influence in the CMA, the possible influence of the foreign-based multinationals should not be overlooked. Membership dues, assessed on the basis of the annual sales and number of employees of a company, are the sole source of financial support for the CMA.

Since most of Canada's manufacturing industries belong to at least one group which represents their interests, the number of groups involved is considerable. The following discussion focusses on a few of the interest groups in this category in order to provide some idea of the diversity in the characteristics and interests of the groups.

The Air Industries Association of Canada represents 120 manufacturing companies, large and small, of aerospace products. As the member companies export most of what they produce, the Association's foreign policy goals focus on trade issues. Within the federal government, the Association deals most often, although by no means exclusively, with the Departments of Industry, Trade and Commerce and National Defence, in support of lowering tariff and non-tariff barriers for aerospace products and securing competitive financing to compensate the industry for the relatively low level of military spending in Canada. When issues of vital concern to the industry arise, the Association and its member companies independently approach the government. The Air Industries Association of Canada relies entirely on membership dues for its funding.

The Canadian Nuclear Association represents over 200 companies and organizations interested in the development of nuclear energy. Its principal goal is to promote a climate conducive to the acceptance of nuclear energy for peaceful purposes. In the area of foreign policy, its chief concerns revolve around the marketing abroad of Canadian nuclear products and services. It operates through standing committees, one of which is devoted to international relations. In addition to maintaining regular contacts between its Toronto headquarters and the federal government, the Association produces publications, hosts conferences and seminars for members and government officers, and lends articles on the latest developments in the industry. It is financed primarily by the membership fees paid by its 160 voting members, based on the size and involvement of the companies. In addition some revenue is generated by the sale of publications and by conference activities.

Canada is a producer, exporter, and importer of textiles. Most of the domestic industry is based in Quebec, although some is located in Ontario. There are several prominent textile associations in Canada, each of which is funded by its membership. The diversity of interests which exists among these associations is best exemplified by the Canadian Textile Importers Association, which advocates lower tariffs to reduce the cost of imported goods in Canada, and the Canadian Textiles Institute, which seeks to protect the domestic industry from foreign competition. The Canadian Textiles Institute represents 150 textile manufacturing companies across the country. Its major goals are the promotion of exports and the protection of domestic markets from foreign imports of textiles or apparel. In support of these objectives, the Institute makes representations to the government with regard to bilateral trade relations, GATT (General Agreement on Tariffs and Trade) negotiations – especially those pertaining to the Multifiber Agreement – and to creating an international trade framework conducive to the health of Canada's textile industries. Other associations representing various sectors of Canada's textile and clothing industries generally advocate protectionist policies. These groups include the Canadian Apparel Manufacturers Institute and the Shoe Manufacturers' Association of Canada.[8]

The Textile Trade Association seeks to reconcile some of the goals of the Canadian Textile Importers Association and the Canadian Textiles Institute, as its membership includes Canadian importers, converters, and manufacturers of textiles. The Textile Trade Association represents 51 firms which supply textiles to Canada's apparel industries. Given the potentially conflicting interests of its heterogeneous membership, the Association approaches the government regularly to promote trade policies which balance the interests of both the domestic manufacturers and the importers of textiles.

The Shoe Manufacturers' Association of Canada is a national organization, with two affiliated provincial associations, which represents 105 manufacturers of footwear and handbags. Foreign trade policy is a high priority for the Association although it is also concerned with issues pertaining to the International Labour Organization and with international social conditions. The work of the Association is funded primarily by membership fees.

The Association of Consulting Engineers of Canada represents 850 firms, both large and small, across Canada. Since its members sell $350,000,000 to $400,000,000 worth of services abroad annually – some 20 per cent of their total sales – its main foreign policy related goal is the promotion of export trade. The Association is concerned with Canada's policies on international employment standards and towards the World Bank and international lending agencies, as these organizations generally provide the money to pay consulting firms. In addition, Canada's policies on foreign aid and on the funding of projects overseas affect the international operation of consulting companies. The Association is financed by its membership.

In addition to the above-mentioned associations, other manufacturing groups include the Confectionery Manufacturers Association, which is concerned with international commodity trade, the Canadian Chemical Producers' Association, which is active in petrochemical trade policies, and the Automotive Industries Association, which is concerned with bilateral negotiations pertaining to the auto pact with the United States.

Unlike those of the other members of CBIIAC, the interests of the Canadian Association – Latin America and Caribbean and the Canadian Committee of the Pacific Basin Economic Council are geographically focussed. Both groups seek to promote trade and business opportunities between Canada and their designated regions.

The Canadian Association – Latin America and Caribbean promotes Canadian economic and business involvement in Latin America and the Caribbean. This involvement includes joint ventures, investment, and trade, although it is primarily concerned with Canadian exports to the area. In support of its foreign policy goals, CALA makes representations to the federal government, sponsors and is represented at international conferences, holds seminars and bilateral committee meetings in Canada, and takes trade missions abroad. While priority is accorded to its foreign policy goals, CALA also develops awareness within Canada of business opportunities in Latin America and the Caribbean.

CALA's membership includes approximately 250 to 260 corporations, of widely varying size, with interests in the region. In addition, every provincial government is a member. The Association is financed by membership dues calculated according to a company's size and its current or potential involvement in the area. In addition, the Canadian International Development Agency (CIDA) provides some funding on a contractual basis for industrial co-operation projects.

The Canadian Committee of the Pacific Basin Economic Council is the national umbrella group for companies engaged in trade with the non-communist Pacific rim countries. Its membership is composed of 150 executives representing 60 to 70 corporations, most of which are incorporated in Canada. The Canadian Committee is a member of the international organization, the Pacific Basin Economic Council, which facilitates multilateral consultation among business people in the countries involved. The Canadian Committee has several objectives: to strengthen the free enterprise system; to improve the business environment, both domestically and internationally; to maintain existing, and generate new, business opportunities; and to increase international trade, especially exports and the level of investment. In support of these objectives it represents Canadian business interests in the region at international conferences and promotes greater public awareness within Canada of relations with the Pacific Basin. It also provides Canadian companies with information on developments in the Pacific Basin and assists them in establishing and expanding business activities in this area. The Committee is the official private sector adviser to the Canadian government on relations between Canada and the Pacific region. While its membership is drawn from across Canada, the Committee tends to be concentrated in Ontario, Quebec, and British Columbia. Its work is financed by its membership.

There are several financial associations of note in Canada which are involved in foreign policy issues, the principal ones being the Canadian Bankers' Association and the Association of Financial Corporations. The Canadian Bankers' Association represents all schedules A and B banks in Canada. The CBA's policies are set by its members in committees, which report to an executive council. While most of its work focusses on domestic issues, the CBA is involved in several areas of foreign policy. It co-operates with the Bank of Canada to influence Canada's position on the International Monetary Fund and with the Standards Council of Canada to try to ensure that Canada's position at the International Organization for Standardization is in the best interests of Canadian bankers. The Association works with the Department of Justice in determining the latter's approach to the Task Force on United Nations Groups which establishes international principles concerning such topics as bills of exchange and promissory notes. In addition, the CBA is heavily involved in the activities of the International Chamber of Commerce. It nominates the Canadian representative to the ICC's Commission on Banking Techniques and Practices and provides the secretariat for the Canadian Working

Party on the Commission. The Commission establishes uniform practices, procedures, and rules for banking operations in the area of documentary credits, collections, and contract guarantees. Most of the CBA's operations are conducted out of its national office in Toronto, although several divisions are located in Montreal. The Association has 130 full-time employees and is funded by membership dues which are pro-rated according to a bank's assets.

As the mining industry produces in excess of the domestic market demand, it is dependent on exports for its economic viability. As a result, all of Canada's major mining groups are concerned about the international economic environment and access to foreign markets, both of which are affected by government policies.

The Mining Association of Canada has a membership of between 87 and 90 firms which represent 95 per cent of the total productive value of Canada's mining sector. The goals of the Association centre around the promotion of exports, especially to large markets in the United States, the European Communities (EC), and Japan. The MAC approaches the federal government with respect to policies, both domestic and foreign, which affect the economic viability of the industry. In terms of foreign policy, the Association advocates the negotiation of trade agreements which require further processing of concentrates within Canada. The Association has also been active in the law of the sea negotiations on deep seabed mining, in terms of both making representations to the Canadian government and having a representative on the Canadian delegation to the Third United Nations Conference on the Law of the Sea.

There are two other major national mining groups in Canada: the Prospectors and Developers Association, which represents junior mining companies involved at the early stages of production; and the Canadian Institute of Mining and Metallurgy, which is a technical and professional body representing individual mining engineers. There are also provincial mining associations in Ontario, Quebec, and British Columbia and regional chambers of mines. All these groups work to ensure the health of the mining industry in Canada and advocate government policies conducive to increased exports.

Another important resource sector is that associated with forest products. While there is a national organization, the Canadian Pulp and Paper Association, groups representing the various industries involved with forest products tend to be regionally based. The Canadian Pulp and Paper Association represents 54 pulp and paper manufacturing companies from across Canada. These companies produce a wide range of products, 75 per cent of which are exported. Given the importance of foreign trade to the industry, the Association makes submissions to the federal government with regard to import and export policies. The work of the Association is funded by membership fees which are based on a percentage of production at the mill.

The Maritime Lumber Bureau is a regional organization representing the four Atlantic provinces. Its 250 members are lumber producers, equipment suppliers, and other related businesses. As 43 per cent of the lumber production of its members goes to foreign markets, the Bureau has an ongoing interest in export promotion. In support of this goal, the Bureau works closely with the Department of Industry, Trade and Commerce and arranges trade missions to foreign markets. The executive director of the Maritime Lumber Bureau represents eastern Canada at European conferences and at the International Organization for Standardization meetings in the USSR. The Bureau is funded by membership dues and provincial government grants.

The Nova Scotia Forest Products Association, which represents the entire forest industry in the province, has foreign policy goals pertaining to the maintenance and promotion of markets for forest products, both in the United States and overseas. While the Association does not handle the marketing directly, it acts in an advisory capacity and keeps members informed of any possible new markets or requests for forest products. The Association has between 550 and 600 members in three categories. Active members consist of lumber companies, sawmills, pulp and paper mills, hardboard mills, Christmas tree producers, pulp wood contractors, and woodlot owners. Associate members are usually individuals interested in the industry. Affiliate members tend to be companies which service or sell goods to the industry. Although the Association is based in Nova Scotia, it keeps abreast of national and international concerns through similar organizations in other parts of the country and through contacts with the provincial and federal governments. It derives its funding from membership dues and from administration fees for the access road building programme.

There are two principal organizations representing the petroleum industry in Canada: the Canadian Petroleum Association and the Independent Petroleum Association of Canada. The former, as the largest and most prominent representative of the industry in Canada, pursues both domestic and foreign policy goals. The latter confines its activities to domestic issues.

The Canadian Petroleum Association's 66 active members are companies involved in the exploration for and the production of oil and gas. These companies produce over 80 per cent of the crude oil and about 66 per cent of the natural gas in Canada. The Association also has 120 associate members from companies which service the petroleum industry. Canada's foreign economic policies are important to the Association when they affect exports of petroleum. The National Energy Board sets the rates and amounts of oil and gas that can be exported, while the Foreign Investment Review Agency (FIRA) establishes the tariff levels. The Canadian Petroleum Association advocates government policies which will be conducive to foreign exports, including the negotiation of favourable bilateral trade agreements, especially with the United States. The Association is funded by its members.

The fishing industry in Canada is important to the national economy and to communities on the east and west coasts.[9] The Fisheries Council of Canada is a national trade organization which represents 12 provincial associations of companies involved in fishing and fish processing. It also has an associate membership of 130, comprising all the fish processing and offshore trawlers in Canada and some co-operatives, such as the Prince Rupert Processors' Association. The Council seeks to establish direct liaison with fishing industries overseas and to maximize markets, both at home and abroad, for fish and fish products. In its advisory capacity, the Council is able to present its concerns and priorities to the federal government. In terms of foreign policy, the Council advocates the reduction of tariff barriers and the promotion of bilateral trade agreements with the United States, Japan, the EC, the Eastern bloc countries, Spain, and Portugal, all of which fish in Canadian waters. As many of the issues discussed in Committee Two of the Third United Nations Conference on the Law of the Sea are related to fishing, the Fisheries Council of Canada made representations to the federal government and had a representative on the Canadian delegation to the Conference. The Council receives its funding from the provincial associations, which in turn are financed by their member companies.

While the Fisheries Council is the most important representative of the industry, the Canadian Association of Fish Exporters, which represents 37 fish and seafood processors and exporters in Atlantic Canada, shares some of its concerns. Foreign policy goals are accorded top priority by the Association and pertain to bilateral fisheries agreements, multilateral trade agreements, expanding commercial fisheries trade, and the offsetting of EC fish protectionism programmes. In support of these goals, the Association approaches the federal government, in particular the Departments of Fisheries and Oceans, Industry, Trade and Commerce, and External Affairs. The Association is funded by membership fees.

In addition to these national organizations there are a great many other fishing related groups, most of which are organized along provincial or regional lines. Some groups, such as the Pacific Trawler Association and the Atlantic Fisheries By-Products Association, represent companies. Others, such as the United Fishermen and Allied Workers Union and the Nova Scotia Fishermen's Association, represent individual fishermen. All of the fisheries groups listed in this directory have goals related to foreign policy, in support of which they make representations to the Canadian government.

The Seafood Producers Association of Nova Scotia (SPANS) has 22 member companies which operate licensed fish processing plants in Nova Scotia. SPANS approaches the federal government in support of both domestic and foreign policy goals, which are accorded equal priority. Its foreign policy objectives pertain to the conservation and joint management of fish stocks, foreign fishing in Canada's economic zone, and export markets. The work of SPANS is financed entirely through membership fees.

The Fisheries Association of Newfoundland and Labrador Limited represents the interests of the commercial fishing industry in Newfoundland in all its aspects and is a member of the National Body of the Fisheries Council of Canada. Its 26 member corporations are involved primarily in the export business and have a keen interest in all matters affecting trade policy, including tariff and non-tariff import barriers. They are also concerned with Canada's relations with other fishing nations who fish inside the Canadian zone or outside the zone in the North Atlantic Fisheries Organization area. Given its members' interests, foreign policy goals – especially those concerning foreign markets for Canadian products or the conservation and allocation of resources within the zone to foreign fishing nations – are accorded a high priority. In support of its interests the Association approaches the federal government directly and through the National Body of the Fisheries Council of Canada. Membership fees provide the Association with its funding.

The agricultural category includes both business and labour groups. In addition to the fact that some farms are run by corporations, farmers may be considered business people in the sense that they operate to make a profit. Agricultural groups overlap with labour to the extent that workers are hired for a wage by both agribusinesses and individual farmers. In order to consider agricultural interest groups and their particular concerns together, a separate category is necessary.

Agricultural groups can be divided into three subcategories: national organizations, such as the Canadian Federation of Agriculture, which represent farming interests generally; regionally based groups such as Unifarm; and commodity specific groups, such as the Dairy Farmers of Canada. Agricultural groups depend on their members for funding. Given the importance of agriculture to the Canadian economy and the geographic concentration of commodity production within the country, issues relating to farming are politically sensitive. Most agricultural groups have some foreign policy goals, on behalf of which they make representations to the federal government.

The major agricultural interest group in Canada is the Canadian Federation of Agriculture which represents over 200,000 of the country's 300,000 farmers. Its membership is composed of nine provincial federations of agriculture and a wide variety of commodity organizations, including the Canadian Horticultural Council and the Canadian Pork Council. Only two major farming associations are not members of the Canadian Federation of Agriculture: the Canadian Cattlemen's Association, whose main foreign policy interests relate to beef exports to the United States; and the National Farmers Union, which is discussed below.

While macro policy is its main focus of attention, the CFA also makes representations to the federal government with regard to the micro policy level. The Federation advocates the development of orderly market systems, domestically and abroad. In addition, it promotes bilateral trade agreements conducive to increased exports of farm products and supports the Canadian agricultural export legislation at the parliamentary committee stage. On the micro level, the Federation seeks to protect and promote the interests of the individual commodity sectors. Given the importance of exports to the health of Canadian agriculture, the Federation generally supports trade liberalization; however, it also recognizes the needs of some sectors, such as horticulture, to be protected from foreign competitors. In addition to making representations to government, the CFA pursues its foreign policy objectives through its membership in the International Federation of Agricultural Producers. The work of the Canadian Federation of Agriculture is financed by the provincial federations which pay according to the number of farmers and the value of agricultural production in the province.

Philosophical differences exist between the National Farmers Union and the Canadian Federation of Agriculture. The former, which represents approximately 9000 farm families from all provinces except Quebec, operates along the lines of a labour union. It tends to be more willing to engage in confrontation with the government than is the CFA. The NFU advocates the establishment of stable, effective marketing systems and guaranteed equitable prices for agricultural products in order to ensure the economic viability of Canadian farms and dignity for Canadian farmers. Like the CFA, the NFU advocates foreign trade policies which will increase exports and protect domestic producers. The NFU's foreign policy objectives go beyond the immediate economic welfare of Canadian farmers to include global peace, the eradication of starvation, and international development. The NFU urges the Canadian government to adopt policies to support these goals. Most of the NFU's funding comes from membership fees, although it also receives donations and, occasionally, government grants for specific projects.

In addition to their co-operation within umbrella organizations, interest groups in each of the major agricultural sectors work to promote their particular interests. These groups include the Dairy Farmers of Canada; the Canadian Cattlemen's Association; the Canadian Pork Council; the Saskatchewan, Manitoba, and Alberta Wheat Pools; the Palliser Wheat Growers Association; and the Canadian Horticultural Council.

The Alberta, Saskatchewan, and Manitoba Wheat Pools are farmer-owned co-operatives with 57,000, 70,000, and 18,000 active members respectively. The Pools, which function both as viable commercial enterprises and as policy organizations, all belong to the Canadian Co-operative Wheat Producers Limited. While domestic interests are of primary concern to the Pools, foreign policy is accorded a high priority because the Pools are major exporters of grains and oilseeds. Their foreign policy objectives can be classified under five main headings: international arrangements and agreements on grain; market analysis and development; farm inputs and commodities; tariff negotiations and agreements such as GATT; and international development, including 'aid' agreements and technical assistance. The three Pools, jointly and individually, meet with the federal government, on both domestic and international matters. In times of trade and tariff negotiations, their senior representatives are nearly always involved at the ministerial level, in an advisory capacity.

The Palliser Wheat Growers Association represents 2000 wheat farmers in the three prairie provinces. Although priority has been given to domestic policies, the Association is beginning to devote more attention to foreign policy goals. As wheat farmers rely on overseas markets, the Association lobbies the federal and provincial governments for policies that will enable its members to take advantage of these markets. In addition, the Association is concerned that its product, wheat, be used to alleviate starvation around the world. The Palliser Wheat Growers Association is funded by membership fees, donations, and government grants.

The Canadian Horticultural Council is a national organization which provides provincial members with a forum on national issues. It has 61 active voting members and over 45 associate members. The Council, whose membership is composed of producer marketing organizations, provincial departments of agriculture, affiliated national associations, and individual producers, works to protect and enhance the well-being of the horticultural and allied industries in Canada. The Council gives high priority to foreign policy goals which pertain to trade and tariff issues and to foreign investment. In support of these obligations, the Council makes representations to the federal government. It also promotes greater co-operation among those involved in the horticultural and allied industries and increased public awareness of the importance of these industries and of means of using horticultural products. Membership fees and payments for secretarial services provide the Canadian Horticultural Council with its funding.

LABOUR

In 1980, 37.6 per cent of the paid workers outside the agricultural sector and 30.5 per cent of civilian employees in Canada belonged to labour unions.[10] There are several categories of groups representing organized labour. The interests of workers generally are represented by organizations such as the Canadian Labour Congress, a central labour body to which unions are affiliated. Those employed in a particular industry or sector of the economy are represented by such unions as the United Oil Workers of Canada while other unions, such as the Quebec Woodworkers Federation, represent those working in a particular trade. Government employees are represented by such unions as the Canadian Union of Public Employees. Although the provincial organization of the Canadian Labour Congress, the Quebec Federation of Labour, is much larger than the Centrale des syndicats démocratiques or the Confédération des syndicats nationaux, Quebec workers often belong to predominantly francophone umbrella organizations. For example, the Fédération nationale des travailleurs de l'industrie du vêtement is a Quebec-based union with membership in the Centrale des syndicats démocratiques. This trend is attributed primarily to linguistic differences, although the regional nature of the Canadian economy is also an influencing factor.

Many of the labour unions operating in Canada are branches of international unions, usually with their headquarters in the United States. The Amalgamated Clothing and Textile Workers Union represents workers in Canada and the United States and is a member of both the Canadian Labour Congress and the AFL-CIO (American Federation of Labor – Congress of Industrial Organizations). Because the major objective of the unions is to ensure the well-being of the workers they represent in Canada they tend to be less involved with foreign policy issues than are business groups. The degree to which they become involved with such issues depends primarily on the extent to which developments outside Canada affect their members. For example, the Amalgamated Transit Union is unlikely to be involved in the foreign policy making process, while the Canadian Seafood and Allied Workers' Union is concerned about Canada's position on international fisheries negotiations. Its size and resources also determine a union's ability to become involved in international issues beyond the immediate well-being of its members. Canada's largest labour organization, the Canadian Labour Congress, extends its concern for workers to those in other countries, such as Poland. All the labour unions discussed rely primarily on their membership for funding, although some receive government grants for specific projects.

The Canadian Labour Congress, which represents some 2,300,000 workers, is the major organization of affiliated trade unions in Canada. While its primary concerns are domestic – to ensure that working people in Canada have the right to organization and the right through organization to ensure meaningful well-remunerated work – it also has international interests, including the promotion of free trade unionism. Since this is deemed to be possible only in conditions of peace and democracy, the CLC supports efforts towards disarmament. It also promotes economic security, social justice, and balanced, fair trade based on international labour standards. The latter prompts the CLC to oppose the duty-free importation of textiles, not only because they represent a threat to the jobs of Canadian textile workers, but also because they are produced cheaply through the exploitation of Third World workers. The CLC is active in the International Labour Organization and has two representatives on the executive of the International Conference of Free Trade Unions.

The Canadian Labour Congress operates as a federation with a national office in Ottawa, 12 regional offices, one in each province and territory, and 120 local councils. The Ottawa office deals with national and international matters, while the regional and local branches focus on issues within their respective jurisdictions. While the work of the Congress is financed largely by its member unions, it also receives grants from CIDA for some of its development projects.

The newly founded Canadian Federation of Labour is the umbrella group for ten building trade unions which formerly belonged to the Canadian Labour Congress. Together these unions represent over 400,000 workers in the building trades in Canada. The Federation differs from the Congress on two accounts. In the first place, it is politically non-partisan, whereas the CLC supports the New Democratic Party. Secondly, it places greater emphasis on conciliation, rather than confrontation, and advocates co-operation among labour, business, and government representatives to find solutions to the economic problems facing Canada. In addition, the Federation is structured to facilitate maximum co-operation among its members. As a whole it drafts proposals on issues relevant to all its members and the workers they represent. Departments operate within the Federation to enable unions involved in the same economic sectors to decide on policies specifically pertaining to their respective memberships.

The main focus of attention for the Canadian Federation of Labour is economic growth within Canada, which it considers is a prerequisite for full employment, equitable wages and benefits, and social justice. In the area of foreign policy, it is concerned with combatting environmental problems through bilateral agreements, as well as through domestic programmes. One of the Federation's major functions is to represent these interests to the federal government. Its political action programme seeks both to establish good working relationships with federal cabinet ministers and members of parliament and to exert influence at the constituency level. In addition, it strives to increase its members' knowledge of the political system, of the importance of specific issues, and of the advantages and disadvantages of specific policy proposals. The work of the Canadian Federation of Labour is funded by its membership.

Although much smaller than either the Canadian Labour Congress or the Canadian Federation of Labour, the Workers' Benevolent Association also operates nationally. The Association has 6000 members and 100 branches across the country. It operates as a Fraternal Life Insurance Society in which the criterion for membership is the purchase of a policy. Its main goal is to promote a world of 'Peace and Brotherhood.' Members of the Association believe that a country should be ruled by a people's democracy, which would ensure an equitable sharing of the country's gross national product. The main priority for the Association is to remain active in the peace movement and to remain a viable part of Canada's first such peace committee, the Canadian Peace Congress. The Association encourages its members to make their views known to members of parliament, as well as to take an active part in peace committees across Canada. Funding comes from membership fees and donations.

The Confederation of National Trade Unions is the umbrella organization for a wide variety of Quebec labour unions, representing 220,000 workers. While its foreign policy objectives focus on import restrictions to protect jobs within Canada, they also include the promotion of domestic exports and concern for the plight of workers internationally. These goals are pursued through representations to government and through membership in the World Confederation of Labour.

Amongst the unions which are concerned with safeguarding the interests of workers in specific industries or particular trades, the United Automobile Workers of America is an example of the former while the Canadian Air Traffic Control Association is an example of the latter. The United Automobile Workers of America represents 125,000 workers from every province except Newfoundland and Prince Edward Island. As Canada's automobile industry is based in Ontario and Quebec, most of the UAW's members come from these two provinces. The organization's prime objective related to foreign policy is the creation of jobs in Canada through increased sales. This necessitates content provisions for products sold in Canada and better access to markets abroad. The UAW is concerned also about the welfare of workers in countries such as South Africa, Argentina, El Salvador, Chile, and Poland where labour unions are outlawed or harassed. In addition, it is promoting a peace petition which opposes nuclear armament. The work of the UAW is financed by membership dues.

The Canadian Air Traffic Control Association is a national organization with eight regional and 54 local branches. Its 2300 members are individual Canadian air traffic controllers. While domestic interests take precedence, the Association is concerned with the development of the profession on a global scale and with assisting in the upgrading of international labour practices. The Association receives 95 per cent of its funding from membership fees, with insurance, administration, and miscellaneous accounting for four per cent and one per cent respectively.

The Energy and Chemical Workers' Union, a national organization with local unions, represents 35,000 individuals. Foreign policy is part of the Union's continuing day-to-day activity and focusses on the formation of the International Conference on Environmental Future, the establishment of free trade unions internationally, and assistance to unions in developing countries. Membership dues finance the work of the Union.

La Fédération canadienne des travailleurs du textile inc. works to protect and advance the job related interests and economic well-being of its 9200 members. In addition to negotiating collective agreements, the Fédération also gives priority to the establishment of federal government policies which protect the jobs of its members. In support of these objectives, the Fédération presents memoranda and makes representations, in co-operation with the Centrale des syndicats démocratiques, to the federal government. The Fédération is based in Quebec where it works with its affiliated unions at the local level. Membership dues provide the Fédération with its funding.

PROFESSIONAL

While most of the major professions in Canada have national associations to provide services for, and to represent the interests of, their members, they tend to have little involvement in the foreign policy making process. Many professional groups perform regulatory functions, and hence are involved with immigration policies pertaining to the establishment of standards and criteria for admitting foreign members of their respective professions to Canada. The Canadian Council of Professional Engineers has worked, through agreement with the Canadian Employment and Immigration Commission, to facilitate the entry of qualified foreign engineers into Canada.

Several groups are concerned with international issues which directly involve their members. The Canadian Association of Broadcasters and the Canadian Book Publishers' Council make representations to the Canadian government with regard to bilateral agreements, especially with the United States, which affect their respective professions. The Canadian Council of Professional Engineers, which is a federation of provincial engineering associations representing 110,000 individuals, co-operates with the Association of Consulting Engineers of Canada to secure domestic and foreign policies conducive to the export of engineering services.

A few professional groups become involved in foreign policy matters beyond the direct interests of their memberships. The Canadian Bar Association, which has 30,000 members across Canada, advises the Canadian government on some issues involving international law, such as the patriation of the Canadian constitution. Other groups of professionals, such as Professors for Peace in the Middle East, organize to pursue one particular foreign policy objective.

The Canadian Air Line Pilots Association (CALPA) is a national organization representing pilots from seven airlines, with a local organization at each base. CALPA has a total of 16 local councils and 3402 members organized into two categories: members who are active airline pilots and supervisory pilots in the employ of Air Canada, CPAir, Pacific Western Airlines, Nordair, Eastern Provincial Airways, Quebecair, and Air Ontario; and associate members who are active pilots with other airlines. Approximately 35 to 40 per cent of the Association's time is devoted to international aviation concerns. Through its participation in the International Federation of Air Line Pilots Associations, CALPA and other member associations attempt to bring pressures to bear on their national governments and international regulatory bodies to create and maintain the safest possible aviation environment. Of particular concern are maximum daily duty time regulations, medical licensing requirements, and training standards and their enforcement by national governments. Implementation of measures to control hijacking, air piracy, and the transportation of prisoners and dangerous substances are equally important concerns.

The Canadian Air Line Pilots Association maintains informal channels of communication with personnel in federal government ministries and agencies and, from time to time, is invited to participate in Royal Commissions, task forces, and other fact-finding bodies. CALPA derives it funding almost entirely from membership fees.

The Association of Canadian Television and Radio Artists (ACTRA) represents 7000 professional writers and performers in the recorded media. While priority is given to domestic objectives, ACTRA does have foreign policy interests, such as the hiring of foreigners for positions which could be filled by Canadians, on behalf of which it approaches the federal government. ACTRA is a national organization with local branches from British Columbia to Newfoundland. It is affiliated with the International Federation of Actors.

Funding for the Association comes from membership fees, work permits, and administration fees, as well as from collective agreements with producers. Groups within the educational field, such as the Canadian Education Association, tend to have some altruistic foreign policy objectives. The Canadian Federation of Students supports policies favourable to foreign students who want to study in Canada. The Association of Canadian Community Colleges assists its 100 members, which are post-secondary, non-degree granting institutions, to play larger roles in international development. The Association operates a technical assistance proramme, and sends teachers to developing countries as well as bringing students from those countries to Canada. It also takes stands on such issues as the violation of human rights in specific countries such as El Salvador and South Africa. Within Canada, the Association distributes newsletters and editorial materials and holds conferences and seminars to assist its members in their Third World development policies and programmes. The work of the Association is funded by membership fees and, in the case of some of its international projects, by CIDA grants.

The Association of Universities and Colleges of Canada (AUCC) has an International Development Office which focusses exclusively on international development goals. Its programmes include fostering joint projects undertaken by university departments in Canada and in less developed countries, which promote development goals in the latter. The International Development Office has direct access to all Canadian universities and colleges that are members of the AUCC. Most of these universities and colleges have an international liaison officer with whom the Office is in regular and frequent contact. The International Development Office assists Canadian universities in approaching CIDA and the International Development Research Centre, both of which provide funding for inter-university linkages for development and for the work of the office.

CONSUMERS

Consumer groups seek to maximize the overall material well-being of people living in Canada. The principal representative of Canadian consumers is the Consumers' Association of Canada, which works to enhance the standard of living throughout the country. The Association, which has 170,000 individual voting members across Canada, is affiliated with the International Association of Consumers' Union. While most of its energy is directed to domestic activities, the Consumers' Association of Canada has some foreign policy objectives. It opposes import quotas generally and favours greater trade liberalization, in order to lower the cost of imported goods in Canada. While the Association gives priority to the needs of consumers, it recognizes the vulnerability of certain domestic industries to foreign competition and, therefore, supports some protectionist measures for certain commodities. Transnational environmental problems are further sources of concern for the Association.

In addition to representing the interests of consumers to the government and the business community, the CAC conducts research, promotes public education, and publishes the *Canadian Consumer* and *Le Consommateur canadien*. Over 75 per cent of the Association's operating budget comes from membership fees, while the remainder comes from the sale of its publications and from a government grant. While the CAC is the largest representative of consumer interests, it is by no means the only one. The interests of Canadian consumers are protected also by provincial organizations and independent groups, such as the Public Interest Advocacy Centre.

NON-ECONOMIC GROUPS

Enormous diversity exists in the characteristics, goals, tactics, and government contracts of non-economic interest groups. As a result, their abilities to exert influence in the foreign policy making process vary considerably. The work of many non-economic groups suffers from insufficient financial resources and fluctuations in memberships. Interest groups in the veteran/

military support, women's, religious, and ethnic categories usually pursue some goals specifically related to the shared demographic characteristics of their members, although many also have altruistic concerns pertaining to international development, human rights, disarmament, and the quality of the environment. Groups in the citizens' and special foreign policy categories tend to focus exclusively on altruistic goals.

Give the bilingual character of Canada and that generally the Quebec government seeks to play a more active role in international relations than do the other provinces, many of the non-economic interest groups involved in international development and human rights work are organized into two separate entities: one consisting of anglophones and the other francophone members located in Quebec. The two entities often take different positions on an issue. For example, the Consumers' Association of Canada promotes trade liberalization while its counterpart in Quebec seeks tariff protection for manufacturers in Quebec.

VETERAN/MILITARY SUPPORT

Canadian veteran and military interest groups comprise a large, well-organized lobby which makes representations to government on matters pertaining to national defence and the health of the military establishment in Canada. In spite of the size of their collective memberships and the fact that several organizations, including the Conference of Defence Associations and the Royal Canadian Air Force Association, owe their existence to government initiatives, interest groups in this category have had relatively little success during the past decade in influencing government policies.[11] However, they have enjoyed success in changing departmental opinion and action on lower level matters.

Veteran and military support interest groups vary considerably in terms of their memberships, organizational structures, the nature of their interests and goals, and the extent to which they make representations to government. Several groups, such as the Royal Canadian Legion, are prominent and active on the domestic level, but have little involvement in foreign policy issues. The most active groups in the foreign policy making sphere tend to be those representing one particular military sector.

The foreign policy concerns of veteran and military support interest groups encompass a wide range of issues which affect national defence. These include Canada's roles in the North Atlantic Treaty Organization (NATO) and the North American Aerospace Defence Command (NORAD), bilateral relations with allies and potential foes, Canadian imports and exports of military equipment and technology, and questions of disarmament. They also encompass such law of the sea issues as the right of innocent passage, the width of territorial waters, and Canadian sovereignty over the Northwest Passage.

The Conference of Defence Associations (CDA) is the umbrella organization for 10 army groups and for the Canadian Air Defence Officers' Association and the Maritime Defence Association of Canada. The CDA represents some 300,000 serving or retired military personnel. Its principal objectives are to ensure recognition and discussion of the Canadian government's defence policy goals and to advise the government on defence matters. Although in the past attention has been focussed on domestic goals, foreign policy objectives are being given increased weight.

The CDA maintains regular contacts with the Department of National Defence and supports government programmes to increase public awareness of the problems of national defence. The minister of national defence and the chief of the defence staff use the CDA's annual general meeting as a forum through which they report to the country on the state of the armed forces. In addition to hearing guest speakers from other countries and formulating and discussing resolutions, delegates to the annual general meeting receive a confidential briefing from high-ranking defence officials. The CDA has been recognized by the federal government as being the 'voice of defence' and is accorded treatment consistent with that recognition.

The CDA is a national organization. Each of its 12 member associations are national groups with regional branches. The work of the CDA is financed by membership fees, donations, and government grants.

As is to be expected, the primary concern of naval interest groups is naval policy. However, the Navy League of Canada and the Naval Officers Association of Canada also pursue objectives related to foreign policy. The former, which represents over 25,000 Canadians, is concerned with maritime issues as well as with those issues related specifically to naval defence. Through its regular contacts with political and bureaucratic officers of the federal government and through the presentation of briefs, the Navy League of Canada promotes policies aimed at improving Canada's commercial shipping operations, both domestically and internationally, and at increasing the size and capibility of Canada's fishing fleet.

The Naval Officers Association of Canada is a civilian based organization comprising retired naval officers and people serving in the naval reserves. The major concerns of the Association are naval defence and the health of the Canadian navy, although it is interested also in issues pertaining to Canada's military security and to such water-related areas as safety and hypothermic research. It is engaged in ongoing research on the military capabilities of Canada, its allies and its potential enemies, and on issues related to the law of the sea. The recognition of Canadian sovereignty over the Northwest Passage has been an important goal of the Association in recent years, in support of which it attended the United Nations Conference on the Law of the Sea in New York as an unofficial observer. Briefs, prepared by standing committees within the Association, are presented by its president to the federal government. The Association's 2500 members across Canada finance its activities.

The Royal Canadian Air Force Association has a membership of 15,000 people currently serving, or who have served, in the Canadian airforce as well as interested members of the general public. While the Association focusses attention on domestic objectives, it does deal with air defence policy issues which involve Canada's relations with other countries. In approaching the federal government, the RCAFA demonstrates a greater reluctance to present formal briefs and appear before parliamentary committees than do the other veteran and military support interest groups discussed here.

The Canadian Institute of Strategic Studies is a research organization affiliated with York University. The majority of its more than 400 members are academics and individuals who are either serving in or retired from the armed forces. It also draw some members from the business community and from the general public. The Institute works to enhance public awareness and knowledge of all issues which are of strategic importance to Canada. Its foreign policy concerns include disarmament, superpower intervention in the Persian Gulf, armed forces reserves, and Canada's inability to mobilize for anything beyond a very limited, short war. A further source of concern is the fact that both Canada and its NATO allies have focussed on nuclear weapons, for economic reasons, and let their conventional capability slide. In addition, the Institute recognizes the importance of Canada's industrial strategy to its national defence.

In support of these interests, the CISS holds two seminars annually and has met with the minister of national defence and with senior personnel in the Departments of National Defence and External Affairs. It has also made submissions to both the House of Commons and the Senate committees on external affairs and national defence. The work of the Institute is funded by membership fees, sales of its publications, grants from private charitable foundations, government grants, and some donations from corporations.

While virtually all women's groups share a concern for the position of women in Canadian society, some extend their interests beyond Canada's borders, to include disarmament, human rights, international development, and Canada's role in the United Nations. The most prominent women's group in Canada is the National Action Committee on the Status of Women, which represents 200 member organizations from across the country. While the Committee is concerned about the positions of women in other countries, it focusses attention on domestic issues and advocates changes to federal legislation to improve the status of women within Canada.

Match is a national, bilingual organization with a membership of approximately 1100 individuals and 100 associations across Canada. Match directly funds development projects which are initiated and implemented by indigenous women in the Third World with the aim of enabling the projects to become self-sufficient. In addition, it makes representations to the federal government to ensure that Canada's development assistance projects in the Third World involve indigenous women. In order to promote public awareness of its concerns, Match publishes a newsletter and produces other educational materials. The group has extensive contacts with CIDA, from which it receives 75 per cent of its project funding.

Voice of Women is a national organization with 750 members, a few of whom are men, and offices in most provinces. In keeping with its chief objective, the promotion of peace, the group supports nuclear disarmament and opposes increased militay spending and the threat or use of violence. Voice of Women is concerned also with environmental problems, international development, and energy issues. In support of these objectives, the group approaches the government directly and participates in the Consultative Group on Disarmament and Arms Control Affairs. The work of the VOW, which includes publishing a newsletter, organizing seminars, and sponsoring a peace petition, is funded by membership fees and donations.

The Young Women's Christian Association of Canada is financed by its 300,000 members who are organized into 56 local associations in nine provinces and two territories. The YWCA has a broad range of foreign policy goals which it actively pursues. These include international development issues, especially as they relate to women in the Third World; the plight of refugees; human rights violations, with emphasis on apartheid in South Africa; peace issues; environmental problems; and sources and the wise utilization of energy.

The YWCA functions on the local, provincial, and national levels and is affiliated with the World YWCA Council which establishes overall objectives. While the Association focusses its attention on developing greater public awareness within Canada of its foreign policy concerns, it also makes representations to the federal government, largely in the form of briefs. Liaison work with the federal government is conducted out of the national headquarters.

The National Council of Women represents and is funded by 750,000 individuals in provincial and local associations across Canada. It is a non-sectarian, non-partisan movement dedicated to serving the highest good of the family and state. Concern for the highest good results in a wide range of domestic and foreign policy goals. This concern extends to the welfare of women, employment opportunities and standards, human rights, disarmament, international development, environmental protection, and Canada's role in the United Nations. While most of its international work is channelled through the Council of Women in Paris, the NCW also makes representations to the federal government and works closely with CIDA. In addition, the Council seeks to promote public education and to mobilize public opinion in support of its objectives.

The women's groups discussed here tend to have fairly wide ranging foreign policy interests. Other groups choose to focus on one particular issue or area of foreign policy. The Congress of Women and the Women's International League for Peace and Freedom both approach civil servants in the Department of External Affairs in support of policies promoting disarmament. The Canadian Federation of Business and Professional Women's Clubs has been active in supporting the work of UNICEF (United Nations Children's Fund).

Religious groups seek to put into practice the shared beliefs of their members. The Christian churches tend to be the most active religious institutions on issues pertaining to foreign policy and international affairs. Canada's largest established Christian churches – United, Anglican, Presbyterian, Lutheran, and Roman Catholic – and the two main peace-oriented churches – Quakers and Mennonites – all seek input into the foreign policy making process in support of their goals. The more evangelical churches, such as the Baptists and Jehovah's Witnesses, tend to work directly with national churches overseas. Churches themselves cannot be classified as interest groups because they function primarily to maintain a particular belief structure and to perform the rituals which reinforce the belief structure, rather than to represent specific interests. Although internal committees within each church and ecumenical bodies do qualify as interest groups, no clear divisions can be drawn between these groups and the churches themselves. The former are staffed and financed by the churches and have their concerns presented to government officers and to the general public by church representatives.

In pursuing their foreign policy objectives, the church-sponsored interest groups contacted for this study tend to approach the federal government, especially the Department of External Affairs, on a fairly regular basis as issues of concern arise. The degree of interaction with other government departments and agencies depends on the group's goals and the particular issue under consideration. For example, groups concerned with disarmament, with trade and aid, with refugees, or with international development approach the Departments of National Defence, Industry, Trade and Commerce, Employment and Immigration, or the Canadian International Development Agency respectively.

Advocacy work is done on various levels, from letter writing campaigns to fairly regular contacts with civil servants to church leaders presenting briefs to cabinet. Representatives of religious groups tend to interact most often with middle level, government desk officers who are responsible for the relevant area of concern. These officers are regarded as being more knowledgeable in their specific field and more accessible than are more senior government officers.

In preparing briefs for parliamentary committees and presentations to cabinet ministers and members of parliament, church groups are able to draw on their extensive contacts abroad for information. Within Canada, they expend considerable effort on public education and on mobilizing public opinion in support of their objectives. While Canada's major churches have internal committees to consider particular areas of international affairs and extensive links overseas, they frequently pursue their foreign policy objectives ecumenically. Although each church has its own particular beliefs and rituals, the issues at stake are considered to be too important to let differences prevent co-operative action.

The United, Anglican, Presbyterian, and Lutheran churches share wide-ranging foreign policy interests including emergency relief, development aid, trade issues, human rights, and disarmament. The focus for each church, in terms of its primary goals and main geographic regions of concern, varies and each has its own internal body or bodies to deal with foreign policy matters, the principal ones of which are the Committee on the Church and International Affairs (United), the Primate's World Relief and Development Fund (Anglican), Presbyterian World Service and Development, and Lutheran World Relief. All of these churches participate in ecumenical associations and umbrella organizations, such as the Canadian Council for International Co-operation, to further their objectives.

The Canadian Friends Service Committee is dedicated to putting the Quaker 'Peace Testimony,' which advocates the total rejection of violence, into practice. While international peace is the primary goal, consideration is given to human rights, development, justice and refugees, as well as to disarmament. In support of these goals, the Committee publishes *Quaker Concern* and other educational material, and organizes seminars and letter writing campaigns. The work of the Service Committee is funded by the Society of Friends in Canada, which has over 1000 members. The Friends Service Committee co-operates with most of the interchurch groups.

The Mennonite Central Committee (Canada) is the service agency for 69 Mennonite and Brethren in Christ churches in Canada, which together represent some 69,000 people. Although the Committee runs programmes for disadvantaged groups within Canada, and at times advocates policy changes to improve their position, 75 per cent of its time and budget are allocated to its overseas interests. These include development and assistance, relief work, and conflict resolution. The Committee sends experts and skilled personnel, as well as money, to Third World countries to support its development projects. Its relief work involves both the shipping of food and material aid to desperate areas and the bringing of refugees to Canada. As pacifists, the Mennonites and Brethren in Christ believe that problems are best solved without force. In order to promote conflict resolution, the Committee tries to work with both sides in a dispute as a reconciling agency. Within Canada, it promotes greater public awareness of troubled areas and meets fairly frequently with government representatives to bring the Committee's concerns to the attention of foreign policy makers. The Mennonite Central Committee is funded primarily by its member churches, although it does receive matching grants from CIDA for some of its individual projects.

The Canadian Council of Churches represents and is funded by most of the Protestant churches. It functions primarily as a facilitator and co-ordinator of the joint programmes of its members, to promote peace, justice, and human rights. A lack of resources and problems in reaching consensus limit the Council's involvement in advocacy work. However, it does do some liaison work with government officials in Ottawa and at an annual conference on human rights. Through the member churches' network of missionaries working abroad, the Council has access to 'grassroots' information about developments in other parts of the globe, which it makes available to its members, the government, and the general public. The Canadian Council of Churches publishes *Communicator*, a quarterly newsletter.

The Canadian Council of Churches co-operates closely with the Cana-

dian Conference of Catholic Bishops, the national association of Canada's
120 Roman Catholic bishops. The principal objective of the Conference is
the promotion of human rights interpreted broadly to include the right to
enjoy a decent standard of living, as well as the right to justice, to equality,
and to freedom from violence, torture, and arbitrary imprisonment. The prob-
lem of poverty is dealt with on two levels: charity programmes are organized
for the victims; and, increasingly, research is conducted into the systemic causes
of poverty and their possible solutions. Much of the latter research is channelled through ecumenical coalitions, such as the Taskforce on Churches and
Corporate Responsibility. In addition, the Conference approaches government officers directly and writes briefs on a wide variety of concerns. Its publications include the 1979 book, *Witness to Justice: A Society to be Trans-
formed.*

In order to involve the laity, as well as the clergy, in the work of the
church, the Conference established the Canadian Catholic Organization for
Development and Peace. Its 21 members include lay Roman Catholics,
representatives of religious orders, and two bishops. The work of the Organization focusses on aid for international development and for emergency relief.
In addition to raising funds for aid projects in the Third World, the Organization presents briefs to the federal government, organizes public letter writing
campaigns, and promotes public awareness within Canada of the problems
of development and justice which confront people in the Third World. To
this end, it publishes a newsletter, *Global Village Voice*, and produces materials
to be used in school curricula.

In order to minimize the degree of functional overlap the Canadian Conference of Catholic Bishops tends to deal with matters of general policy, while
the Canadian Catholic Organization for Development and Peace focusses on
practical aid. For example, when people are being displaced or fleeing from a
particular part of the world for political reasons, the Conference approaches
the Department of Employment and Immigration with regard to Canada's
policies towards that particular area and towards accepting greater numbers
of refugees. At the same time, the Organization concentrates attention on the
level of aid being sent to help those displaced.

There is a large number of church coalition groups involved in various areas of foreign policy. In general, representatives from the sponsoring churches and ecumenical associations sit on the administrative committee of each inter-church group and provide a channel for two-way communications. The coalition groups work both through their sponsoring organizations and independently.

The Taskforce on Churches and Corporate Responsibility is financed by its 10 institutional members which include the major Canadian churches, religious orders, the Canadian Council of Churches, and the Canadian Conference of Catholic Bishops. The Taskforce is concerned with corporate conduct in areas of the world where violations of human rights and social justice occur. The regions of greatest concern are Southern Africa, Latin America, and Central America. The activities of companies operating within, or having extensive commercial relations with, countries known to violate human rights are assessed according to whether they are contributing to the creation of an environment more conducive to the protection of human rights or whether they are reinforcing an oppressive régime. In raising questions about the social impact of business decisions with Canadian corporations, banks, and government, the churches speak as shareholders as well as major social institutions in the country. Denominational members of the Taskforce urge corporations and banks to adopt a role which corrects socially unjust situations. They support such private sector endeavours.

The group's members meet with senior management of private sector enterprises about specific policy issues. They also have contact by telephone and correspondence with government officials, MPs, and on occasion meet with relevant ministers. Several submissions have been presented to parliamentary committees. The issues concern legislation dealing with the formulation or enforcement of laws relevant to corporations or banks and their accountability to the Canadian public or their impact on socially disadvantaged groups. Their contacts have taken place primarily with the Departments of External Affairs, Industry, Trade and Commerce, and Finance.

A significant number of business people who are active in their respective churches object to the work of such groups as the Taskforce on Churches and Corporate Responsibility on the grounds that it is undertaken without the benefit of a thorough understanding of business operations and of international commerce. The Confederation of Church and Business People agrees with the generic foreign policy objectives of the churches, but objects to the tactics chosen to pursue these goals. By contributing a business perspective, the group seeks to assist the churches in formulating objective, pragmatic policies. The Confederation is a national organization with volunteer units and 900 members across Canada. Its work is funded by its members and by corporate donations.

Citizens for Public Justice, also known as the Committee for Justice and Liberty, is a national organization with some 2000 members and with regional affiliates and local groups. Like the church taskforces with which it co-operates, Citizens for Public Justice is interdenominational. The group seeks to put the Christian principles of freedom, justice, peace, compassion, and stewardship into practice. Priority is given to domestic concerns, such as the development and implementation of responsible economic growth, energy, and social and human rights, especially for native peoples. However, it does have foreign policy interests such as the promotion of human rights and meeting the legitimate needs of poor people in Third World countries. Citizens for Public Justice urges the Canadian government to adopt foreign policies which will help ensure justice for all people and help establish the practice of stewardship by all. It also conducts research, promotes public education on issues relevant to its concerns, and produces several publications and a weekly radio programme. The work of Citizens for Public Justice is financed by membership fees, individual donations, church offerings, and subscriptions.

There is an increasing concern amongst religious communities over issues of peace and security. Numerous peace groups have emerged at congregational levels. Generally, they share a common perspective and employ similar tactics. Their philosophies stem from religious doctrine, are deep-rooted, and focus on man's stewardship over the planet earth. These groups are opposed to the nuclear arms race and its threat to human survival. Linkages are made between the waste in human, physical, and financial resources involved in military production by the developed nations and the problems of underdevelopment in the Third World. Their goals are wide-ranging and include the need to encourage a stronger Canadian effort to achieve a comprehensive nuclear test ban, the desire to implement the strategies of nuclear suffocation and a nuclear freeze, and the adoption of a no-first-use resolution on nuclear weapons. They are in opposition to the cruise testing decision and hope to prevent further defence testing arrangements of this nature. Finally, they would like to see Canada declared a nuclear weapons free zone.

The Christian Movement for Peace is an international, ecumenical organization concerned with conflict resolution and justice. Disarmament issues are the priority for the Canadian branch which has 600 members, most of whom live in Ontario. The Christian Movement for Peace conducts research and promotes greater public awareness of its concerns by organizing seminars and study trips, providing resources for study groups, assisting other religious groups to organize workshops, and producing materials to be used in school curricula. In addition, it publishes *Calumet* and participates in the international work camp programme. While the Movement channels most of its government liaison work through Project Ploughshares, it does participate in the Consultative Group on Disarmament and Arms Control Affairs. Funding for the group comes from the major churches, private donations, fund-raising activities, and CIDA grants.

Project Ploughshares, which began as a research project, is now a national organization with a membership of 15 sponsoring organizations and over 7000 individuals. It is classified as a religious group because of its close working relationship with churches and because most of the people involved in its work have church affiliations. However, several of its sponsoring organizations, including Oxfam and the United Nations Association, are not religious groups.

Project Ploughshares gives top priority to its foreign policy goals in support of which it approaches the federal government. Disarmament and arms control are key objectives for the group, which advocates economic conversion policies to shift resources from defence to civilian industries and budget shifts from defence to development. It also promotes a move away from a dependence on weapons of mass destruction to the use of alternative means of ensuring security. Project Ploughshares promotes a more independent foreign policy for Canada, especially in terms of its relationship with the United States. The termination of the defence production sharing arrangements is advocated so that Canada would no longer be obliged to follow the broad dictates of the United States or to regulate its military exports to other countries according to their relationships with the United States. A further concern is the link between armaments and underdevelopment. Disarmament is desirable not only for the promotion of peace, but also for the re-allocation to development of resources currently spent on arms. Project Ploughshares is funded by the churches and other sponsoring organizations, by income from projects, by donations and contributions from individuals, and by CIDA grants for disarmament-and-development work.

Obviously, the religious peace groups have a broad set of objectives coupled with the recognition that the struggle to re-orient Canadian security policy is a long-term project that will be measured in terms of decades rather than months or years. Their tactics reflect their philosophy and objectives. Educational outreach programmes, the preparation and presentation of briefs to government officials, and letter writing campaigns to members of parliament are of equal importance, while participating in mass demonstrations is gaining legitimacy.

Both the Inter-Church Committee on Human Rights in Latin America and the Inter-Church Committee for Refugees receive their financial and staff support from major Canadian churches and religious organizations. The former promotes human rights in Latin America through co-operation between churches in Canada and in Latin America and among Canadian churches in their work to protect human rights. It brings human rights violations to the attention of Canadian Christians, the government, and the general public, in order to generate support for its work. The Committee monitors and assesses Canada foreign policies in terms of their contributions to the promotion of human rights and advocates policy changes when necessary. In support of its foreign policy objectives, Committee representatives approach members of parliament, both individually and in committee, while church leaders make presentations to the secretary of state for external affairs and the prime minister.

The Inter-Church Committee for Refugees addresses both the plight of current refugees and the economic, political, and military conditions which cause people to become refugees. Priority is accorded to combatting the forces of violence and repression which operate in many areas of the world. The Committee recognizes the importance of Canadian foreign policy to the promotion of world peace and to the success of its work. Government policies determine the amount, type, and geographic destination of development aid and the numbers and national origins of the refugees who are allowed to immigrate to Canada. The Committee advocates that the Canadian government develop policies to enable larger numbers of Latin American refugees to settle in Canada and to promote peace and a greater sharing of global resources among all peoples.

The World Conference on Religion for Peace (Canada) is a national branch of the World Conference on Religion for Peace, an international organization of leaders of most of the world's major religions who co-operate to promote world peace. The Conference serves as an example, especially to political leaders, of the possible existence of harmonious relations among peoples of diverse beliefs, and communicates concerns to those in power. The Canadian branch advocates gradual disarmament, beginning with nuclear arms, and stresses the need for Canada to conduct more research into, and play a larger role in, global diplomacy. It is a participant in the Consultative Group on Disarmament and Arms Control Affairs. The Conference promotes public education in Canada and publishes a newsletter. It has 300 paying members from most of the provinces and from nine religious bodies. Membership fees, donations from church and religious bodies, and government grants for specific projects provide the Conference with its funding.

ETHNIC

There are large numbers of ethnic groups in Canada, reflecting the country's multicultural heritage.[12] Internal divisions, such as those found in the Chinese and Ukrainian communities, and the diversity of issues on which they choose to focus prompt many ethnic communities to sponsor several interest groups.

Ethnic groups tend to give priority to the welfare of their members in Canada and to Canada's relations with their respective countries of origin. Some groups are involved also in a broad range of foreign policy concerns, including human rights, international development, peace, and bilateral agreements ensuring direct flights between Canada and their original homelands.

In support of these goals, ethnic groups approach a wide variety of government officials.

The Jewish community in Canada is particularly well-organized and well-represented. Its three major groups are the Canadian Jewish Congress, which is the principal co-ordinating organization, B'nai B'rith, which is a service agency and consequently has little direct involvement in foreign policy issues, and the Canadian Zionist Federation, which co-ordinates and finances bilateral social and cultural programmes. These three organizations jointly established the Canada-Israel Committee which focusses entirely on relations between the two countries.

The Canadian Jewish Congress represents, and is financed by, the Jewish lay community which numbers 300,000. It is concerned with humanitarian issues and human rights, especially for Jews, and works to keep Jews and the general public aware of issues affecting the Jewish community internationally. The CJC functions as a federation with its national headquarters in Montreal and five fairly independent regional branches across Canada. Its priorities and general policies are developed at a triennial plenary assembly.

In addition to speaking for the Jewish community on all issues involving Canadian-Israeli relations, the Canada-Israel Committee co-ordinates activities among Jewish organizations dealing with this area of foreign policy and produces several publications. The Committee promotes public education on issues dealing with relations between Canada and Israel and organizes trips to Israel for politicians and academics. The Canada-Israel Committee, which is funded by the Canadian Jewish community, has offices in Ottawa, Montreal, and Toronto.

The Canadian Arab Federation is a national organization which represents and co-ordinates the activities of 22 Arab associations in Canada. The Federation has four main foreign policy objectives: that Canada's foreign policy be independent from that of the United States; that Canada's support for the United Nations Charter be reflected in an objective policy on the Middle East, reflecting Palestinian rights in the Holy Land; that Canada seek to reduce tensions among the superpowers; and that Canada stay outside of military pacts. In support of these goals, the Federation presents briefs, makes presentations, and sends letters and telegrams to the federal government. Its work is financed through membership fees, government grants, and donations. The Arab Palestine Association is a local organization with a mandate to speak on behalf of all Palestinian-Canadians in Canada. The Association promotes greater understanding of the plight of Palestinians and supports Palestinians and Arabs in their struggle to achieve their national rights and independence. The Association approaches the federal government directly in support of these interests. The work of the Arab Palestine Association is funded by membership fees from its 1000 individual members, donations, and by income from sales and social events.

The Association of United Ukrainian Canadians is a national organization comprising primarily, but not exclusively, farmers and workers of Ukrainian descent. Its foreign policy objectives include multilateral arms reductions, the resolution of conflict through political discussions, increased social, economic, scientific, and political contacts between democratic and communist countries, the rights of workers everywhere to organize and to enjoy a decent standard of living, and the right of self-determination for all states. In addition to its 4000 to 5000 active, paying members, the Association has a wider group of supporters. Its financial resources come from membership fees, donations, and fund-raising activities.

The Canadian Polish Congress is the umbrella organization for 250 to 260 Polish associations in Canada. In addition to its domestic concerns, the Congress represents the Polish community in Canada on issues of international politics, especially those concerning Poland. In light of recent events in Poland, the Congress advocates that the Canadian government take an active stand in opposing the continuation of martial law, work for the release of political prisoners, increase the number of refugees admitted to Canada, and recommend that a solution to the crisis be worked out jointly by Solidarity, the government, and the church.

CITIZENS

Citizens groups primarily comprise individuals who, regardless of their economic or demographic characteristics, co-operate in the pursuit of common goals. Many of these groups, such as the National Survival Institute, also have members which are associations. Citizens groups vary enormously in their organization, resource orientations, tactics, and interests. For simplicity, and to permit the identification of groups working in the same policy areas, they will be classified, according to their primary foreign policy interests, under four main headings: international development, human rights, environmental, and peace issues. Citizens groups generally pursue their foreign policy objectives through direct approaches to the federal government and through public education. In addition, some maintain contacts with groups which share similar concerns in other countries.

There is a significant number of groups concerned with international development. Some, like Oxfam and the YMCA of Canada, support development assistance projects for peoples in various Third World countries, while others, such as the Canadian Hunger Foundation, focus on one particular type of issue, or on one particular category of persons, as does UNICEF in its work to relieve the sufferings of deprived children in developing countries.

Although Oxfam-Canada promotes public awareness of international development issues in Canada and sponsors some domestic projects, especially for native peoples, activities abroad are its main focus. These include the promotion of human rights, assistance to refugees, and the relief of hunger, poverty, and political repression. It organizes and sponsors assistance programmes overseas, especially in the form of self-help projects in South Africa, the Caribbean, and Latin and Central America. It is concerned also with the overall social and economic situations in the countries where it operates and, increasingly, makes representations to the Canadian government in favour of tougher policies towards repressive régimes and of recognition for certain liberation movements. In addition, Oxfam-Canada opposes increases in defence spending which divert resources from development projects and are associated with military dictatorships.

Although most of Oxfam's relations with the federal government are conducted through its national office in Ottawa, it also has regional offices in six cities across Canada, each with its own staff, board of directors, and local committees. Quebec has its own organization, Oxfam-Quebec. The regional offices of Oxfam-Canada operate fairly independently in establishing their own projects and policies; however, they do meet every two years to discuss issues and to facilitate co-operation. Each regional branch sends representatives to the national committees and boards in Ottawa.

Oxfam-Canada has 2000 members who volunteer their time to serve on committees of its national and local bodies. It receives donations from 20,000 individuals and some matching grants for specific projects from CIDA and from four provincial governments.

Oxfam-Quebec operates independently. Like Oxfam-Canada, it is concerned with the problems of underdevelopment. However, it does not become involved in advocacy work but confines its activities to promoting greater public awareness within Quebec of these problems and to supporting development assistance programmes in Latin America, Africa, and Asia. Oxfam-Quebec has 180 members and a staff of five paid employees and 25 volunteers.

The Canadian University Service Overseas promotes international solidarity by providing volunteer workers and support for Third World development projects. Cuso recognizes the importance of Canada's international development policies to these projects, and hence seeks input into the policy-making process. A single executive board administers the organization, although it has two fairly autonomous branches, each with its own structure and programmes. The English-speaking branch has its main office in Ottawa. Montreal is the headquarters for the French-speaking branch, Service universitaire canadien outre-mer (Suco), which has 25 institutional and 100 individual members. Cuso's work is financed by an annual CIDA grant, donations, and contributions from the countries in which its projects operate.

World University Service of Canada has its secretariat in Ottawa, a regional office in Montreal, and volunteer local committees on college and university campuses. Its membership includes 61 universities and colleges and 250 individuals who are students, faculty, and administrators at post-secondary institutions, secretariat personnel, and other professional overseas workers and returned volunteers. WUSC is affiliated with World University Service International and its primary concern is the development goals of the countries with which it works. Its main foreign policy objectives are to assist developing countries in realizing their educational goals and to foster an interest in and concern for international understanding among the Canadian academic community and the general public. Funding for WUSC comes from membership fees, donations, grants from CIDA, the Department of External Affairs, and Marches des Millions, and from Caravan sales.

World Vision Canada, a 'support office' for World Vision International, is an autonomous national organization which shares in the support and direction of the international body. World Vision Canada has 94,000 active donors and sponsors and four regional offices across Canada, in addition to its national headquarters. While the group is concerned with domestic issues, priority is given to foreign policy goals. World Vision Canada is committed to international development through self-help community programmes and leadership development. As a result, the group supports the goals and purposes of the North-South dialogue and Canada's role in it. It does not support tied aid which forces a nation to accept Canadian goods and services in return for Canadian aid. A related concern is the position of the Canadian government in recognizing other governments, especially when non-recognition undermines the ability of non-governmental organizations (NGOs) to alleviate suffering.

World Vision Canada also supports disarmament and condemns the stockpiling of nuclear and other arms, both as a threat to international peace and harmony and as a misallocation of resources which could otherwise be used to alleviate suffering. The extension and broadening of Canada's refugee policies are other areas of concern for World Vision Canada which has assisted refugees in Africa, Asia, and Latin America. In support of these objectives, the executive director of World Vision Canada has, on numerous occasions, expressed concern directly to the prime minister, leaders of the opposition, the secretary of state for external affairs, and provincial premiers. Some recent issues of concern have been supporting an expanded refugee policy, opposing food sanctions against Poland, and urging Canada to speak out against the Israeli invasion of Lebanon. World Vision continues to be active in the standing conference on refugees and has participated in a number of dialogues with government. In addition, it promotes public education on underdevelopment, appropriate development, and the role that Canada can play. The major portion of World Vision's funding comes from the private sector, although since 1975 the Canadian government has become a significant source of income for World Vision Canada.

The YMCA is an international organization with 90 national movements and 10,000 local associations. In 1982 the YMCA of Canada had 1,020,661 individual members. Its National Council comprises representatives of 75 local, autonomous associations. The Council promotes an integrated approach to Canadian foreign policy, which takes into account the realities of an interdependent world. Its specific foreign policy concerns relate to Canada's role in global negotiations, development assistance, East-West relations, and disarmament. The National Council of YMCAs of Canada approaches the federal government directly in support of these objectives at the invitation of the policy-makers and when such an approach is considered useful and appropriate. Programme and membership fees provide the Council with 71.6 per cent of its funding, while most of the rest comes from revenues raised in campaigns and operations, and from grants from all three levels of government.

The prime function of UNICEF Canada is fundraising for UNICEF's programmes to promote the welfare of children in developing countries. In addition, the national branch is involved in public education and in seeking increased government aid for UNICEF's work. The international UNICEF headquarters in New York is responsible for the overall establishment of priorities and the co-ordination of funds and projects. The national office, located in Toronto, works in liaison with the international headquarters and with the provincial and local committees within Canada. It also represents the interests of the organization before the Canadian government. Most of UNICEF Canada's funds and activities are channelled through the international office. However, the national office directly funds some overseas projects. The organization receives its funds from the government through CIDA and through fundraising from the general public, most of which is done at the local level. In addition to the 2500 individuals who serve on its committees, UNICEF Canada has 35,000 to 40,000 volunteer workers.

Inter Pares is a small but active group in the field of international development. Its 50 members include politicians, business people, and interested individuals from across Canada. Inter Pares promotes international development, through channelling assistance to projects in the Third World and through advocacy work directed at both the federal government and the general public. The group examines the various aspects of Canadian foreign policy that affect the quality of the country's development assistance. These include policies on trade, tariffs, and immigration, as well as on aid. On questions of development assistance, Inter Pares has direct contacts with CIDA, although it also approaches the Department of External Affairs and members of parliament, both individually and in committees. On energy issues, the group contacts CIDA and the Department of Energy, Mines and Resources.

As public support is deemed necessary for policy changes, considerable attention is paid to developing public awareness of North-South issues and of Canada's relations with Third World countries. Inter Pares produces materials to be used in school curricula and organizes workshops for teachers and school board officials. The work of Inter Pares is financed by private donations and by matching grants from CIDA for specific projects.

The World Federalists of Canada is a national organization with branches in many centres across the country. Most of the organization's 1200 active and 200 inactive members are individuals, although a few groups also belong. Foreign policy goals are given top priority. These goals are concerned with reform of the United Nations, and disarmament, international development, the environment, and human rights issues. The World Federalists approach the federal government in support of their foreign policy objectives. The work of the group is financed primarily by membership fees, although some funds come from donations and from occasional government grants.

While there is widespread recognition of the link between human rights and international development, especially if the former is interpreted broadly to include the right to a decent standard of living, some interest groups focus on the protection and promotion of human rights. Some of these groups, such as Amnesty International, have worldwide concerns, while others, such as the Toronto Committee for the Liberation of Southern Africa, concentrate on one particular region. Given the importance of Canadian foreign policy to their work, most of these groups make representations to the federal government. In addition, they tend to be actively involved in public education.

Amnesty International is an independent human rights organization. Its headquarters in London, England, co-ordinates its overall work and distributes information to its national associations. The Canadian Section of Amnesty International has two branches, one English-speaking and one

French-speaking. Within these branches, local groups do the practical work to fulfil the organization's mandate. The English-speaking branch, based in Ottawa, has 93 such groups and a total membership of 10,000. Montreal is the headquarters of the French-speaking branch which has 37 groups and 4000 members.

Prisoners are the focus for Amnesty International's human rights concerns. It works for the release of those who have neither employed nor advocated violence but who are imprisoned because of their beliefs, colour, sex, language, religion, or ethnic origin. Prompt and just trials are sought for all political prisoners and the use of torture and the death penalty are unconditionally opposed. In support of these goals, members of Amnesty International's executive, select committees, and local branches make representations to the federal government.

In order to maintain its autonomy, Amnesty International does not accept government money for its ongoing work, although it does receive government grants for some special projects. The organization is financed by membership fees and by individual donations and subscriptions.

While generally less well known than Amnesty International, the Canadian Human Rights Foundation also promotes international human rights principles, although its focus is domestic. Other groups concentrate on various categories of people, such as certain minority groups or refugees, and on various parts of the world. For example, the 500 members of the Toronto Committee for the Liberation of Southern Africa support those liberation movements in South Africa and Namibia which seek full political and civil rights for the non-white population and the efforts in Zimbabwe and the former Portuguese African colonies to reconstruct society according to socialist principles.

There are several other interest groups which seek to assist the victims of racial discrimination in Southern Africa. These include Canadians Concerned About South Africa, the International Defence and Aid Fund for Southern Africa (Canada), and the Southern Africa Action Coalition. Other groups are concerned with Canada's policies towards refugees. In the case of the Vietnamese refugees – the 'boat people' – Operation Life Line actively encouraged the Canadian government to accept larger numbers. In contrast, the National Citizens Coalition opposed the admission of the refugees. Canada's policy towards the Middle East is the focus of concern for at least one citizens group. The Middle East Discussion Group is a national group, although its membership and activity is largely concentrated in Ottawa. The Group's 100 members include parliamentarians, academics, former officials of the Department of External Affairs, and journalists, virtually none of whom have ethnic or commercial ties with the Middle East. The Group focusses almost exclusively on ensuring that Canada adopt an effective policy towards the Middle East. For most members that entails a policy less biased in favour of Israel and more sympathetic to the Palestinians. The philosophy of the Stanfield report on the Middle East is supported by most of the Group's members. The Middle East Discussion Group has met with the prime minister and with the secretary of state for external affairs. In addition, it has sent statements to the secretary of state for external affairs and has participated in several House of Commons luncheon meetings, at irregular intervals. To date, no membership fees or donations have been solicited by the group and any operating expenses have been met by the individuals.

In response to greater public awareness of and concern about environmental problems in the last 15 years, the number and significance of environmental groups has increased. These groups tend to pursue their objectives through direct contacts with the government, especially Environment Canada, and through public education.

As is the case with other citizens groups, those involved in environmental issues vary considerably in size and composition of membership, interests, tactics, and relations with government. Pollution Probe's members are individuals while both individuals and associations are members of the Canadian Nature Federation. The interests of Great Lakes Tomorrow tend to be geographically focussed, while those of the National Survival Institute are more broad-ranging. The Canadian Wildlife Federation has close ties with Environment Canada while Greenpeace frequently seeks to influence government policies indirectly by generating media and public support for its objectives. Some interest groups, such as SPEC, are regionally based, while others, such as Energy Probe, are national.

The main umbrella organization for environmental groups is the Canadian Nature Federation which works to promote wildlife conservation and solutions to environmental problems. In addition to its 87 affiliated environmental and conservation groups, it has 18,000 individual members. The Federation's foreign policy concerns focus on transboundary pollution – especially the problems of acid rain, bilateral water diversion projects, migratory wildlife, and pipeline construction – and therefore involve Canada-United States relations. In addition to presenting the interests of its membership to the federal policy-makers, the Federation is involved in public education and publishes *Nature Canada*. The work of the Federation is financed by its members.

The National Survival Institute is a coalition of individuals and organizations in Canada concerned with the quality of the environment, both domestically and internationally. The Institute tends to focus on the macro-policy level and interprets the environment broadly to include such diverse issues as sources and uses of renewable energy and the status of women, as well as pollution problems. It is concerned also with the inter-relationship between the Canadian and global environments. In support of these goals, the National Survival Institute seeks input into the Canadian foreign policy making process and promotes public education, domestically among other voluntary organizations and the general public and in liaison with international bodies concerned with environmental issues. While most of the Institute's budget comes from membership fees and individual donations, it also receives some project grants from corporations and the federal government.

One of the most prominent forerunners in the environmental field is Pollution Probe, a national organization with 1000 individual members. Although based in Toronto, Pollution Probe pursues environmental concerns across the country. While domestic interests are the focus for its work, the impact of developments in one part of the world on the quality of the environment globally is recognized. As a result, Pollution Probe has recently become involved in two main areas of international relations: the environmental hazards posed by toxic chemical wastes from abandoned dumps along the Niagara River, including the Love Canal; and the use of pesticides, such as DDT, in developing countries. Although the use of these pesticides has been banned in North America, they are still being manufactured here and exported to the Third World where they are sprayed without proper precautions onto food which is exported to North America. Pollution Probe condemns this practice not only because of the health hazards it poses for agricultural workers in developing countries and for the consumers of the contaminated food but also because of the dangers it poses for the environment. An additional concern with foreign policy implications is acid rain. Pollution Probe was a founding member of the Canadian Coalition on Acid Rain which is currently lobbying in Washington, DC, for tougher emission standards.

In support of its objectives, Pollution Probe makes representations to government, co-operates with other environmental groups, both in Canada and abroad, and promotes public education to rally support for and action on environmental issues. *Probe Post* is sold nationally and internationally. Of Pollution Probe's $285,000 budget in 1982, $100,000 came from membership fees and individual and corporate donations. The remaining $185,000 was derived from contract work, the sale of publications and services, and some government grants.

Because of its success in capturing media attention, Greenpeace is one of the best known environmental groups. Its foreign policy goals can be categorized under two broad headings: the protection of endangered species, especially whales and seals; and safeguarding the quality of the environment, with particular attention to the threat posed by nuclear energy. Local branches of Greenpeace may choose to address additional concerns; for example, the Ontario branch is concerned with acid rain pollution. Greenpeace has over 50,000 members in Canada and is funded primarily by donations and membership fees.

In addition to the interest groups which are concerned with the quality of the environment generally, some groups choose to focus on a geographic region, as does Great Lakes Tomorrow, on issues pertaining to a specific area of concern, as does Energy Probe, or on a particular species, as do Ducks Unlimited and the International Atlantic Salmon Foundation.

Great Lakes Tomorrow is a binational organization based in the Great Lakes Basin. It seeks to increase citizen participation on both sides of the border in decisions pertaining to the Great Lakes. The group has a membership of 50 and a board of directors of 24. As the effective management and control of the Great Lakes requires the co-operation of both Canada and the United States, foreign policy goals are important to the group. Great Lakes Tomorrow seeks commitments from the governments of both countries to restore and rehabilitate areas of the Great Lakes which have been polluted and otherwise degraded and, subsequently, to maintain ecologically sound standards. Great Lakes Tomorrow works with governmental institutions, such as the International Joint Commission, and co-operates with environmental groups. It also works to increase public knowledge of and input into the policy-making process on issues pertaining to the Great Lakes. It receives its funding from membership fees, donations, and government grants.

Energy Probe is a national organization which promotes a sound Canadian energy policy, both at home and abroad. Internationally, it is opposed to the export of nuclear and coal produced electricity to the United States for ecological reasons, and to the sale of nuclear equipment and technology to the Third World on the grounds that such sales are detrimental to global harmony. In addition, Energy Probe is concerned about the fact that the industrial countries are consuming a disproportionate amount of energy, which leaves fewer resources for Third World development. Energy Probe has 15,000 supporters, of which 10,000 are in Ontario. It is funded by donations and membership fees.

Ducks Unlimited Canada is a national organization with 19,000 individual members and provincial and local offices. It is affiliated with Ducks Unlimited organizations in the United States, Mexico, and New Zealand. As waterfowl breed in Canada and winter in southern North America and South America, the welfare of these birds during their migration abroad is very important to Ducks Unlimited Canada. The group pursues foreign policy objectives pertaining to the Ramsar Convention, the Migratory Bird Treaty, and the North American Waterfowl Management Plan. The work of Ducks Unlimited Canada is financed by membership fees and donations.

The International Atlantic Salmon Foundation is an international organization which is formally incorporated in the United States and in Canada. Its 1500 members include both individuals and organizations. The Foundation's foreign policy goals pertain to the management of harvests and the conservation of Atlantic salmon, and related research. Highest priority is given to ensuring effective, international management of the harvesting of salmon from distant waters, in order to guarantee the maximum survival of that fish species at sea and on its return to the rivers of its home country. In support of these interests, the Foundation approaches governments in Canada and abroad, both directly and indirectly. Funding for the Foundation comes from donations and membership dues.

Many Canadians are concerned about the dangers of war, especially of war involving nuclear weapons, and have organized interest groups to promote global peace. For most of these groups disarmament and arms control are crucial objectives. All of the groups discussed below, except the Canadian Peace Congress, participate in the Consultative Group for Disarmament and Arms Control Affairs.

Science for Peace is a national organization with 250 members from across Canada. The group is concerned about the danger of war, fought either with nuclear arms or with weapons of mass destruction. In order to lessen this danger, Science for Peace urges the Canadian government to support the establishment of an international peacekeeping satellite system which would report to the United Nations, to oppose the testing of cruise missiles, and to reexamine Canada's relationships with its NATO allies to ensure that they are in the best interests of national and international security. Through participation at international scientific conferences on the problems of nuclear security, the group seeks to promote improved East-West relations. Education, both of its members and of the general public, is an important objective for the group. Science for Peace publishes a newsletter and is responsible for the establishment of the first Canadian Chair of Peace Studies at the University of Toronto. The work of the group is funded by its members.

Operation Dismantle is a national organization with 1300 members in branches across Canada. Its ultimate aim is to have a worldwide referendum on disarmament organized by the United Nations General Assembly. It urges the Canadian government, therefore, to propose a global referendum on disarmament to the General Assembly and seeks to mobilize public support within Canada in favour of disarmament. With the support of Mayor Dewar of Ottawa, Operation Dismantle launched a campaign to have disarmament questions included on the ballot in the 1982 Canadian municipal elections.

Approximately 59 city and town councils decided to put the issue to their constituents. By mobilizing public opinion through municipal referenda, Operation Dismantle hoped in the first instance to show that an overwhelming majority of Canadians want a real start on disarmament, and in the second to bring attention to the proposal for a worldwide referendum on disarmament.

The Canadian Peace Congress is a national organization with over 4000 members and 27 local councils across Canada. The Congress's peace objectives fall under several headings. The main focus is the promotion of disarmament and of a more independent foreign policy for Canada. Peace is interpreted broadly to include human rights and justice, both of which are considered prerequisites for global harmony, and international development, whose progress could be accelerated if it received the money currently spent on arms. While some local councils have membership fees, most do not and the majority of funds for the Canadian Peace Congress come from voluntary contributions. Internationally, it is affiliated with the World Peace Congress.

In addition to those mentioned above, there has been a phenomenal growth in the formation of 'grassroots' peace groups, at the national, provincial, and municipal levels. In Toronto and Vancouver alone there are some 250 active groups. There is an increasing tendency for such groups to band together in coalitions to maximize their political effectiveness and to pool their resources.

SPECIAL FOREIGN POLICY

The members of special foreign policy interest groups, like those of citizens groups, are not drawn together because of demographic or economic characteristics. Special foreign policy groups can be divided into two broad subdivisions: umbrella organizations whose members are institutions or associations; and groups with close links to the academic community, for whom research is the primary focus. While both types interact at times with representatives of the federal government, they put considerable emphasis on studying developments in their specific areas of international relations and on informing their members and the general public of their findings.

Special foreign policy umbrella groups exist in several areas of foreign policy, including international development, energy issues, and disarmament. There is some potential for overlap between groups in this category and those classified as citizens groups because some in each division have both individuals and associations as members. The decision on where to place umbrella groups with mixed memberships was based on the proportion of the mix. Groups with predominantly individual members were classified as citizens groups, while those whose memberships comprised primarily associations and institutions were placed in the special foreign policy category.

The Canadian Council for International Co-operation is the major umbrella group for Canadian voluntary agencies interested in increasing Canada's commitment to international development. The Council distributes information to and helps co-ordinate the joint activities of its 90 member organization. Information is circulated also to its 75 individual members.

The Council's major foreign policy objectives relate to international development, with particular emphasis on the level and quality of Canada's foreign aid. It is concerned also with Canada's trade policies, which can either enhance or undermine the country's contribution to international development and the role which voluntary agencies are able to play in international development programmes. The promotion of human rights is a further objective of the CCIC. The Council deals on both the macro-policy level, as exemplified by its general concern over Canada's relations with Third World countries, and on the micro-policy level, as exemplified by its opposition to apartheid. The CCIC presents its concerns and objectives before the government, the media, and the general public.

The Association québécois des organismes de coopération international is the umbrella organization for the Quebec member associations of the Canadian Council for International Co-operation. Like the latter, the AQOCI promotes and facilitates the work of its members and, when necessary, represents their interests before government bodies, other organizations, and the Quebec public.

Many of the concerns of the CCIC and the AQOCI are shared by the Canadian Coalition for a Just Economic Order, an organization which seeks to ensure that Canada's foreign policies are conducive to the establishment of a New International Economic Order.

Friends of the Earth is a national federation of 21 environmental groups which co-operate in promoting conservation and in bringing environmental problems to the attention of policy-makers and the general public. Although domestic issues continue to be the main focus of the group, international issues, especially those related to the export of Candu reactors and of coal-produced electricity, are becoming increasingly important. In addition to its representative function, Friends of the Earth publishes *Alternatives: Magazine for Friends of the Earth* and *FOE Newsletter*, distributes publications related to environmental concerns, and participates in international conferences. The work of the group is funded by membership fees, donations, and government grants for specific research projects.

Another umbrella group active on environmental issues is the Canadian Arctic Resources Committee, a well-organized national group with 20 members which approaches the federal government in support of policies to safeguard the environment, especially in the far north.

The Conservation Council of Ontario is a provincially based organization which promotes the conservation, rehabilitation, and most effective use of soil and water resources and of the life which they sustain, in order to enhance the welfare of all. The Council has a membership of 33 organizations, including the Ontario Federation of Labour and the Consumers' Association of Canada, and 110 individuals. Its constituency numbers over one million.

While priority is given to domestic concerns, the Conservation Council has foreign policy objectives pertaining to immigration, transboundary pollution, and management of the Great Lakes. The Council has contact with several federal ministers and members of parliament, the Cabinet Committee on Resource Development, and leaders of the opposition parties. In addition, it has participated in government committees and taskforces. It encourages co-operation among environmental groups and between these groups and government agencies. It also promotes research and public education. The work of the Conservation Council of Ontario is funded by membership fees, donations, and government grants.

In order to achieve their goals, environmental groups may co-operate on specific projects, such as Energy for Development. This project is the first coalition of energy and development groups, including Energy Probe, Friends of the Earth, and Inter Pares, which seeks to link the two issues. Energy for

Development both informs the educators and presents policy proposals to government officials. The work of the coalition is funded by donations from individuals and the sponsoring organizations and by matching CIDA grants.

The Canadian Forestry Association is a federation whose membership is drawn from nine provincial forestry associations, representing over 10,000 people, as well as 50 individuals. The Association is concerned with all issues related to the management of forests and promotes co-operation among those involved in this area. Its 17-member board of directors includes one representative from each of the provincial forestry associations and representatives from various sectors concerned about forest management: labour, the media, various levels of government, academics, and business people. The Association makes representations to the federal government with regard to international and bilateral agreements affecting forest management. These would include agreements on such issues as mutual aid in fighting forest fires. It also promotes public education on the wise use of Canada's forest, water, soil, fish, and wildlife resources. The work of the Canadian Forestry Association is funded by donations from national business and financial organizations and by grants from the federal government.

While interest groups in the second subdivision of the special foreign policy category are all involved in research, the focus of their interests varies. For example, the Canadian Institute of International Affairs is interested in virtually all aspects of international relations, while the Conference Board of Canada focusses on economic issues and international trade.

As a private, non-partisan organization, the Canadian Institute of International Affairs provides a forum for discussion of and objective research into international affairs and Canadian foreign policy. These studies enable the Institute to transmit information and analysis to government officials, to its members, and to the general public. In addition, the Institute facilitates contacts between the government and academic/professional and business communities in Canada. The CIIA organizes conferences, study trips, and seminars, and maintains a library specializing in materials on Canadian foreign policy and international affairs. The Institute's publications include *Behind the Headlines* and *International Journal*, as well as books, bibliographies, and pamphlets on international affairs.

The CIIA is a national organization with programmes and publications for both English- and French-speaking Canadians. It has 25 branches located in cities across Canada and one in New York City. Donations from individuals, foundations, and corporations provide the CIIA with its financial resources.

The North-South Institute conducts in-depth policy-relevant research on relations between industrialized states, primarily Canada, and developing countries. In order to increase awareness of the Third World and its importance to Canada, the Institute makes its research findings available to government officers, other groups working in the area, and members of the public. The Institute's research also enables it to evaluate Canada's programmes in the area of international development, particularly those related to aid and trade, and, subsequently, to make policy recommendations. Canada's aid programmes are assessed in terms of their success in accomplishing the government's stated goals. Canada's trade links are examined primarily in terms of which regions are markets for Canadian exports and sources of Canadian imports. To date the research has concentrated on the macro level of analysis.

The overall direction for the North-South Institute is set by its board of directors, while its daily operations are carried out by a staff of 30. The Institute receives its funds from private foundations, book sales, and fees for government contract studies. Because the Institute is neither an umbrella group nor a member of any other organization, it is free to assess the work of other groups and associations, as well as that of the government.

The United Nations Association in Canada functions primarily as a public information centre, distributing written materials, including its quarterly *Bulletin*, and providing speakers on key international issues. It conducts studies and promotes public education on matters with which the United Nations is concerned – international development, disarmament, and human rights – and on Canada's role as a member of the United Nations.

Although it does little direct lobbying, the Association does take stands on issues by passing resolutions at its annual meeting. These are then sent on to the appropriate government department, normally the Department of External Affairs. Apart from these written resolutions and an annual meeting with the secretary of state for external affairs, there is not normally an attempt to pressure the government with regard to any particular issue. The

Association has, over the years, supported various initiatives on an informal, relatively low-key basis.

The United Nations Association in Canada is a national organization with its headquarters in Ottawa and 2650 individual members. In addition, 22 Canadian organizations pay a nominal fee to be national affiliates in return for which they receive information services. Branch offices in cities across Canada organize meetings, seminars, and conferences, and act as resource centres for their regions. The work of the UNA is funded by membership fees, individual and corporate donations, the sale of information services, and government grants, either on a sustaining or on a project basis.

In 1972 the Quebec sector of the United Nations Association in Canada established a separate organization, L'Association québécois pour l'avancement des Nations-Unies. Like the UNA, this group promotes public education in international development and in the creative role which the United Nations and its agencies exercise in this area. The AQANU organizes conferences, seminars, study trips, and a summer training programme in the Caribbean. Its publications include a bulletin and a journal. The AQANU has approximately 500 members of which the majority are drawn from the educational community in Quebec. The organization is financed through public funding, especially in the form of CIDA grants, membership donations, and fund-raising activities.

The Canadian Study Group on Arms Control and Disarmament is a national organization which conducts in-depth studies of issues pertaining to arms control and disarmament, primarily to enable its members to develop comprehensive, balanced views of the subject. A representative of the Group is invited biannually to participate in the Consultative Group on Disarmament and Arms Control Affairs in Ottawa.

The Study Group holds monthly meetings in Toronto to discuss relevant issues. The minutes of these meetings are sent to its 50 members, who include representatives of the relevant federal government departments, business people, and academics. Funding for the Group comes from a grant from the Department of External Affairs. This money is administered by the Canadian Institute of International Affairs which also provides the Group with office space.

CONCLUSION

While this study has produced some findings concerning the numbers, characteristics, and activities of interest groups involved in foreign policy issues, it was never intended to be a general analysis of how these groups function. Nevertheless, some observations can be made about the nature of groups and their role in the foreign policy making process. The almost 200 interest groups identified in the survey represent a considerable cross-section of the Canadian population. They have been classified into eleven categories according to the primary basis of affiliation of their members. Interest groups whose primary goals are the economic well-being of their members include business, agricultural, labour, professional, and consumers groups. Those with primarily non-economic goals include veteran/military support, women's, religious, ethnic, citizens, and special foreign policy groups.

The number of organizations that can from time to time become involved in lobbying the Canadian government on issues pertaining to foreign policies is far beyond the scope of any one study. To cite just two examples, policies dealing with imports and exports of commodities affect, either directly or indirectly, virtually all industries and, indeed, all companies in Canada; if the Canadian government decided to halt immigration, most ethnic groups would protest to Ottawa. Under less drastic circumstances many of these groups would focus their energies on social and cultural activities within their own communities. While many groups work to maintain ongoing relations with the federal government, lobbying activities vary in intensity and in numbers of participants. Since it is usually easier to have an influence when policy is being made, rather than after it has been in place for some time, groups tend to seek input during the formulation of policy. For example, representations by the business community increase when the federal government is formulating its policies for the next round of negotiations under the General Agreement on Tariffs and Trade.

Interest groups surveyed here tend to be institutionalized, in the sense that they have established relations with bureaucratic and political decision-makers in the federal government and they maintain permanent offices with telephones and staff. These groups also tend to be the largest and most active in foreign policy issues on an ongoing basis. Many civil servants consider CBIIAC and its seven number associations to be the most important groups with which they deal on matters pertaining to trade, commerce, and financial issues.

Information about non-institutionalized groups is much more difficult to come by because they often lack permanent addresses, telephone numbers, and contact persons. Many citizens groups, such as the Canadian Committee for the Relief of Biafran Refugees, are formed on an ad hoc basis to deal with a particular issue or crisis and cease to function once that issue is resolved or the crisis becomes less acute. In some cases, these groups become institutionalized over time. Some interest groups, particularly those representing ethnic communities, have frequent changes of address, not only because of frequent moves but also because of the practice of using the current president's address for the group's correspondence. When the president changes, so does the mailing address.

Not only are there a large number of diverse interest groups involved with foreign policy issues but many have heterogeneous interests. Business groups such as the Canadian Export Association are concerned with foreign aid policies as well as with issues directly relating to foreign trade and the general business environment. Many 'peace' groups interpret peace broadly and have foreign policy goals which extend beyond disarmament to include human rights and international development. Heterogeneous interests may reduce the resources which a group can devote to any one issue. However, since these interests are often perceived to be complementary and interrelated, a gain in one area is considered an improvement in the group's overall postion. Pollution Probe, for example, opposes the export of hazardous pesticides to developing countries. Success on this issue would not only help to protect the natural environment but would also improve the working environment of agricultural workers in developing countries. In so doing, it would help to protect the health of Canadians since, in many cases, they are the consumers of agricultural products that are grown in the Third World with the use of hazardous pesticides and then exported to Canada. On this issue, Pollution

Probe's goals of protecting both the environment and the health of individuals in Canada and abroad are complementary.

The heterogeneous interests of many groups quite often result in the involvement of diverse groups in a particular issue. For example, some groups within each of the categories of labour, women's, citizens, religious, ethnic, and special foreign policy are concerned with human rights. Amnesty International, the Taskforce on Churches and Corporate Responsibility, the Canadian Jewish Congress, and the United Automobile Workers of America are all concerned about the denial of human rights in Argentina, although the focus of their concern differs. Amnesty International is interested in the rights of political prisoners who have never advocated or employed violence. The UAW, on the other hand, is concerned about the harassment of organized labour.

There is a considerable communications network among many interest groups. In the business community, the creation of the Canadian Business and Industry International Advisory Committee suggests the extent to which co-operation is possible. Executives from many of Canada's largest corporations and business organizations meet regularly through CBIIAC to discuss issues of mutual concern. They make joint representations to the federal government on foreign policy issues, when it is possible and advisable to do so. But because the member organizations of CBIIAC have differing interests as well, they also approach the government individually. Among religious coalition groups too there is a significant communications network and a considerable overlapping of memberships. For example, a staff member of the Canadian Conference of Catholic Bishops, Bernard Daly, also chairs the Inter-Church Committee for Refugees. As its name would suggest, Energy for Development is sponsored by a coalition of energy groups, such as Energy Probe, and development groups, including Inter Pares.

The wide range of foreign policy issues pursued by interest groups indicates the number and diversity of the issues which foreign policy embraces. Collectively, the groups surveyed are concerned with international trade and economics, aid and development, arms control and disarmament, human rights, environmental, and other issues. Each category encompasses several subdivisions. For example, trade and economic issues include not only Canada's export and import policies but also policies on multinationals, investment, and finance. They involve Canada's bilateral policies as well as its position at international conferences, such as the GATT negotiations, which seek to establish regulations to govern international trade.

The fact that foreign policy objectives may be complementary indicates the interrelationship which exists among foreign policy issues. Many of the groups which view disarmament as the road to greater peace and security contend that the money which is currently spent on arms could be redirected to promote international development. For these interest groups, the goals of world peace and international development are complementary.

In other cases, the foreign policy objectives of one interest group may conflict with those of another. The business organizations that seek to promote Canadian exports are concerned about freer competition in world markets. They tend to believe that prices for exports, including technology, should be set by market factors. Many of the non-economic groups that seek to promote international development consider technology to be an important resource which Canada should share with developing countries. These groups argue that political agreements on the transfer of technology are vital to speeding up the pace of development in the Third World. The business organizations that represent the owners of technology contend that such transfers through government intervention disrupt world markets for technology. Conflicts over goals can also occur within an interest group, thereby reducing its effectiveness in certain areas. The Canadian Export Association, for example, did not play a major role in the Tokyo Round of the GATT negotiations because of disagreement among its members over priorities for negotiating tariff reductions with the European Communities, Japan, and the United States.

The structure and organization of interest groups in Canada tend to reflect the political, economic, and linguistic realities of the country. The federal structure of government provides interest groups with multiple access points at the national, provincial, and municipal levels. In order to take full advantage of these points, interest groups often develop internal structures parallel to those of the federal political system. Many groups with economic interests, such as the Fisheries Council of Canada and the Canadian Labour Congress, have both national headquarters and provincial offices. Given the resources needed to establish and run a national office and provincial offices, the federal option is simply not available to all groups. Nevertheless, some non-economic groups, such as the YWCA of Canada, UNICEF, and the Canadian Forestry Association, have federated structures.

For the most part, the interest groups surveyed do not make representations to provincial governments on foreign policy issues since these issues are usually considered to be the preserve of the federal government. Representations to provincial governments are, of course, made in connection with domestic policies. From this one could conclude that a federated structure is less salient to the nature of interest group representation in the foreign policy making process than it is to representation in the formulation of domestic policies. Nevertheless, some interest groups, such as the Canadian Friends Service Committee and the Canadian Importers Association, do, on occasion, approach provincial governments on matters pertaining to foreign policy. This is obviously done in the hope of getting provincial support for a particular policy position.

The desire to cultivate access points at various levels of government is not the only reason for establishing provincial offices. Because of linguistic differences and the fact that the Quebec government tends to be more active in some aspects of international affairs than are the other provincial governments, some national groups in most of the eleven categories have fairly autonomous English- and French-speaking branches. The Swiss Canadian Chamber of Commerce and Amnesty International are examples of such groups. In addition, there are totally independent groups which represent similar categories of English- and French-speaking Canadians. La Fédération nationale des travailleurs de l'industrie du vêtement represents approximately 6000 French-speaking textile workers. In English-speaking Canada, these interests are represented by such unions as the Amalgamated Clothing and Textile Workers Union.

The organization of interest groups is also influenced by the structure of regional economic activities in Canada. Many of the groups involved with resource sectors, especially the fishing and forestry industries, are organized regionally. For example, the Atlantic Fisheries By-Products Association and the Pacific Trawler Association represent companies, on the east and west coasts respectively, which are involved with the fishing industry.

The structure of the Canadian parliamentary system offers multiple access points for interest group lobbying: the cabinet, the civil service, the Senate, advisory committees, royal commissions, taskforces, regulatory agencies. Many interest groups have cultivated specific contacts within the government but are understandably reticent to divulge these contacts, although they are more willing to disclose the points at which they seek access. But even this information is usually kept confidential. This can be seen as evidence for the contention that groups which want to maintain relations with governmental actors, especially bureaucrats, must keep such relationships confidential.[13] Nonetheless, the representatives who are willing to discuss their points of contact in the federal government tend to cite cabinet ministers and civil servants as the most sought-after targets. Cabinet ministers in particular are generally considered the key actors to approach when the issues at stake are of major importance. This finding substantiates those of other writers in the field.[14] Although less frequently cited, parliamentary committees, especially the House of Commons Standing Committee on External Affairs and National Defence, are also points of access. In virtually all cases, groups will seek access at several points.

Among civil servants and interest group representatives, there is a general perception that the Canadian system is becoming more open and that the cultivation of public support is becoming increasingly important to effective lobbying. Other analyses of interest groups have drawn similar conclusions about interest group behaviour on domestic issues in Canada.[15] With very few exceptions, representatives of groups within each category were willing to discuss their goals and activities. They also expressed an interest in being included in the survey. However, this openness was by no means pervasive, and several group representatives were reticent to discuss certain areas of their operations, especially those pertaining to budgets.

Canadian interest group representatives often express an aversion to the term 'lobbying.' There would appear to be two main reasons for this concern. First, groups with charitable tax status risk losing it if they lobby the government. Given the expenses incurred by interest groups and the importance of charitable tax status for raising funds, this concern is understandable. Beyond this practical consideration is a pejorative connotation which the term 'lobbying' has for many. Frequently 'lobbying' is seen as conniving to exert undue, or perhaps even improper, influence. On the other hand, there seems to be no aversion to 'involvement' in foreign policy issues.

While the policy-making system may be opening up, many group representatives feel frustrated in their attempts to have government officers take their views seriously. Group representatives will, on occasion, specify instances in which their respective groups have been able to affect the shaping of policy. In general, however, most perceive their influence to be fairly small. Even business groups, which are frequently portrayed as exercising disproportionate influence, complain that government is insensitive to their needs. Foreign policies pertaining to the transfer of technology, the National Energy Program, and the Foreign Investment Review Agency are often cited as examples of areas in which business interests are not heeded.

The extent to which an interest group will be successful in influencing the foreign policy making process depends on a variety of factors, including its access to key governmental decision-makers, its perceived legitimacy, the nature of its demands, the timing of its requests, the tactics it chooses, and the resources at its disposal. Perceived legitimacy is a key factor in securing both access to and influence with governmental policy-makers. Bureaucrats and politicians are much more amenable to representations to alter policies in a modest and incremental way than to demands which run counter to the general direction of government policies. Thus proposals from, say, major Canadian banks on the negotiation of freer international trade in computer services receive a quite different hearing in official circles than do proposals from major church groups on trade with South Africa. From a policy-maker's perspective, Canada cannot overnight simply shift its position, for example, on NATO or on nuclear weapons. Demands which more closely mirror the government's priorities are much more likely to succeed. Similarly, tactics which support the government will be viewed much more positively than will those that embarrass it.

Financial resources constitute a group's single most important asset.[16] Money can, of course, be used directly in an attempt to influence the policy-making process through campaign funds to candidates and to the political party or parties most likely to succeed at the election polls. Although the recent tightening of disclosure and auditing regulations for campaign funds has increased the degree of 'probity, openness and equity' in the system, election expenses continue to be high.[17] Perhaps more commonly and importantly, adequate financing enables interest groups to develop the structures, expertise, permanence, tools, and commodities to bargain more effectively in several arenas.

The financial resources and the sources of funding of the interest groups surveyed vary considerably. For 1982, Pollution Probe had a budget of $285,000. In the same year, the Mennonite Central Committee's budget was $8 million, most of which was to be spent on its projects overseas. Some 'ad hoc' groups have miniscule, if any, budgets. Non-profit groups which have charitable status are required by law to provide audited financial statements. On the other hand, the exact financial situation of other interest groups is often unclear because they are reticent to disclose details about their finances. Nevertheless, certain conclusions can be drawn as to the financial resources of interest groups from their membership and the nature of their operations. The Canadian Manufacturers' Association has over 8300 corporate members, with permanent offices and paid staff in Toronto and Ottawa. The CMA's financial resources are obviously far greater than are those, for example, of the Canadian Study Group on Arms Control and Disarmament which has 50 individual members, no office, and no paid staff.

In general, interest groups rely on their members to provide a significant amount of funding. This is usually collected through membership dues and the sale of publications and services to members and others. Most business groups receive all their financial support from this source. Many of the non-economic groups, such as the Canadian Institute of International Affairs, rely on donations from private foundations and corporations to augment their financial resources. Government grants are a further source of revenue for certain groups. Inter Pares and the National Survival Institute, for instance, receive government grants for some specific projects.

The relationship between government and interest groups is symbiotic. Groups seek to exert pressure on politicians and on government bureaucrats to ensure that their interests are considered in and furthered by public policies. In turn, interest groups perform some very important functions in the formulation and implementation of government policies. They provide technological information and expertise of use to policy-makers. The Canadian Council of Churches has an extensive network of contacts throughout the world, many of whom send home detailed reports on developments within their specific regions. The Council shares information from these sources with governmental decision-makers, which enables them to be better informed about developments abroad, especially at the 'grassroots' level. Interest groups can also play a significant role in legitimizing government policies. The Canadian government's policies on the issues pertaining to mining the deep seabed were made more credible at home and at the Third United Nations Conference on the Law of the Sea because they had the support of Local 6500 of the United Steelworkers of America, which represented most nickel miners of the Sudbury basin whose jobs could have been negatively affected by unregulated production from the deep seabed.

Interest groups can also provide an important liaison between the government and the people of Canada by aggregating and transmitting public opinions to the policy-makers and by communicating government policies to the people. Most groups produce publications to keep their members informed about issues of importance to them and about relevant government policies. In addition, most groups organize seminars and meetings to inform primarily their members but also the public at large of their concerns. There is an increasing trend among religious and citizens groups in particular to engage in and to promote public education. The Christian Movement for Peace, World University Service of Canada, and Pollution Probe, for instance, are all active in this area. Mobilizing public opinion in support of a particular goal is a recognized means of exerting indirect pressure on the government. Many groups also emphasize the importance of public education as a long-term strategy to create an environment conducive to policy changes.

There is little question that there are large numbers of groups involved in one way or another in the foreign policy making process. It is equally apparent that these groups vary considerably in terms of their internal structure and their heterogeneous interests. The degree to which many groups have interests which span a wide range of foreign policy issues is particularly noteworthy. The involvement of interest groups in the foreign policy making process is a field which offers considerable scope for further study.

NOTES

1   *Toronto Star*, 22 August 1982, p 33.

2   *Ibid*, 18 December 1982, pp A7, A14-15.

3   *Ibid*, p A7.

4   *Ibid*, p A3.

5   See, for example, Richard Gwyn, 'In Ottawa,' *ibid*, 3 April 1982, p C1.

6   Robert V. Presthus, *Elite Accommodation in Canadian Politics* (Toronto: Macmillan of Canada 1973), p 99.

7   The typology used in this survey is based on the one presented by W. Blair Dimock in 'The involvement and influence of domestic interest groups in Canadian foreign policy making,' MA dissertation, Carleton University, 1980.

8   For a more comprehensive listing of these groups, please refer to the Business section of appendix B.

9   The discussion of fisheries groups includes only national and east coast groups because no group representing the fishing industry in British Columbia returned the questionnaire.

10   Canada, Department of Labour, Data Branch, *Directory of Labour Organizations in Canada, 1980*, p 9.

11   Kim Richard Nossal, 'On the periphery: interest groups and Canadian defence policy in the 1970s,' paper delivered to CIIA conference on domestic groups and foreign policy, Ottawa, 9-11 June 1982.

12   In spite of their large number and their potential involvement in foreign policy issues, the ethnic section of the survey is short. Great difficulties were encountered in contacting and eliciting responses from representatives of ethnic groups. This was a result of several factors, including linguistic barriers, frequent changes in addresses, telephone numbers, and executives of the groups, and the fact that many groups do not have the resources to staff an office or to answer telephone enquiries or questionnaires.

13   A. Paul Pross, 'Canadian pressure groups in the 1970s: their role and their relations with the public service,' *Canadian Public Administration* 18 (spring 1975), 131.

14   William T. Stanbury, 'Lobbying and interest group representation in the legislative process,' in William A.W. Neilson and James C. MacPherson, eds, *The Leg-*

islative Process in Canada: the Need for Reform (Toronto: Institute for Research on Public Policy 1978), p 187.

15 Peter Aucoin, 'Pressure groups and recent changes in the policy-making process,' in A. Paul Pross, ed, *Pressure Group Behaviour in Canadian Politics* (Toronto: McGraw-Hill Ryerson 1975), p 173.

16 Richard J. Van Loon and Michael S. Whittington, *The Canadian Political System: Environment, Structure and Process* (Toronto: McGraw-Hill Ryerson 1976), p 300.

17 Khayyam Z. Paltiel, 'Canadian election expenses legislation: recent developments,' in Hugh G. Thorburn, ed, *Party Politics in Canada* (4th ed, Scarborough, Ont: Prentice-Hall 1979), p 109.

BIBLIOGRAPHY

A Balance Sheet of Third World/Canada Relations: Report and Issue-Papers by the North-South Institute. Ottawa: North-South Institute 1979.

BONES, ALAN. 'The Effect of Zionist Interest Groups on Canadian Foreign Policy.' Paper submitted in fulfilment of Political Science 498, Carleton University 1981.

CANADA. Department of Labour, Data Branch, *Directory of Labour Organizations in Canada, 1980*.

CANADIAN COUNCIL FOR INTERNATIONAL CO-OPERATION. *Directory of Canadian Non-Governmental Organizations Engaged in International Development*. Ottawa: Mutual Press Limited 1982.

DIMOCK, W. BLAIR. 'The Involvement and Influence of Domestic Interest Groups in Canadian Foreign Policy Making.' MA dissertation, Carleton University 1980.

Directory of Associations in Canada. Third edition. Toronto: University of Toronto Press 1978.

'A Directory of Toronto Groups Involved in Issues of Militarism, Disarmament and Peace.' Toronto: Christian Movement for Peace 1981.

ENGLEMANN, FREDERICK C., and MILDRED A. SCHWARTZ. *Political Parties and the Canadian Social Structure.* Toronto: Prentice-Hall 1967.

GWYN, RICHARD. 'In Ottawa.' *Toronto Star*, 3 April 1982, p C1.

'The Inter-Church Committee on Human Rights in Latin America.' Toronto: Inter-Church Committee on Human Rights in Latin America nd.

MORRISON, W. ALEXANDER. *The Voice of Defence: the History of the Conference of Defence Associations: the First Fifty Years, 1932-1982.* Ottawa: Department of National Defence 1982.

————— 'The Conference of Defence Associations and the Evolution of the Office of the Major-General Reserves.' MA dissertation, Royal Military College of Canada 1980.

————— 'Major-General A.G.L. McNaughton, the Conference of Defence Associations, and the 1936 N.P.A.M. Re-organization: a Master Military Bureaucratic Politician at Work.' Presented to the 1982 Annual Meeting of the Canadian Historical Association, Ottawa.

NOSSAL, KIM RICHARD. 'On the Periphery: Interest Groups and Canadian Defence Policy in the 1970s.' Paper delivered to a Conference on Domestic Groups and Foreign Policy, Ottawa, 9-11 June 1982.

'Objectives.' Ottawa: Amnesty International nd.

'Position Papers.' Ottawa: Canadian Federation of Labour 1982.

PRATT, BETTE, ed. *Canadian Conservation Directory.* Fourth edition. Ottawa: Canadian Nature Federation nd.

PRESTHUS, ROBERT. *Elite Accommodation in Canadian Politics.* Toronto: Macmillan of Canada 1973.

PROSS, A. PAUL. 'Canadian Pressure Groups in the 1970s: their Role and their Relations with the Public Service.' *Canadian Public Administration* 18 (1) (spring 1975), 121-35.

RIDDELL-DIXON, ELIZABETH M. 'Interest Group Behaviour and the Canadian Policy-Making Process.' PhD qualifying essay, University of Toronto, 1981.

SINCLAIR, HELEN K. 'Matters of Common Concern.' *Canadian Banker* 89 (1) (February 1982), 16-21.

Toronto Star, 22 August 1982, p B3, and 18 December 1982, pp A7, A14-15.

Unesco and Its Contacts in Canada. Report to the Council of Ministers of Education, Canada. Quebec: Quebec Ministry of Education 1981.

WALTERS, SUSAN, ed. *1981 Canadian Almanac and Directory*. Toronto: Copp Clark Pitman 1981.

'Who is my Neighbour.' Toronto: Inter-Church Committee for Refugees 1981.

APPENDIX A
A NOTE ON METHODOLOGY

In conducting a survey of the interest groups involved in the Canadian foreign policy making process the researcher faces several problems of methodology. In the first place, the primary source of data, the interview, is subjective and represents the personal views of the person(s) contacted. Time restrictions and, frequently, the absence of alternative sources of information made it difficult to verify data received. In light of these facts, the discussion of each interest group is confined to information on its purpose, foreign policy goals, membership, structure, and funding. The inclusion of full details on tactics, government contacts, and relative influence and effectiveness of the groups is beyond the scope of this survey.

There are three additional problems related to the use of interviews. Since considerable heterogeneity of opinions and goals is found within many interest groups, the views of the representatives interviewed are not necessarily shared by all the members of their respective groups. In addition, the precise meanings of terms vary from person to person. When asked, several representatives said that their business groups had no foreign policy interests, although they were concerned with issues pertaining to international trade. In this survey, the former is considered to encompass the latter because international trade issues include Canada's export and import policies and the federal government's involvement in bilateral and multilateral trade negotiations.

A few representatives thought that the interview did not provide them with sufficient opportunity to discuss the full range of their group's activities and interests. There is some merit in this criticism. However, the purpose of the survey is to provide some information on a wide range of groups, rather than to present a complete picture of the operations of any one group. As far as possible efforts have been made to present the same type of data on each group.

Secondly, the potential scope of this survey is vast. Foreign policy encompasses a wide variety of issues, ranging from trade to environmental concerns to international development. Likewise, the number of groups involved with foreign policy issues is immense, and, as became clear in the interviews, in most areas of foreign policy whether an interest group was seen as important and active depended largely on the issues under consideration at any one time. These factors made it difficult to determine which groups should be included and what degree of importance should be accorded to each.

The choice of which groups to include was based on several criteria. Efforts were made to include the largest, most prominent groups, several of which are umbrella organizations for other groups. Groups which were considered important by and had working relationships with the government officials interviewed generally were included, as were groups which were mentioned consistently as being active by the umbrella organizations and other groups involved in the same area of foreign policy. While recognizing that some groups indirectly influence government policy through mobilizing the support of the media and the general public, the study was focussed on groups which approach the government directly. Finally, for budgetary reasons the interviews tended to be geographically concentrated on groups with offices in Ottawa and Toronto. As a result of these limitations the initial draft of the paper was over-representative of institutionalized groups.

In order to reach relevant groups in other parts of the country and those previously overlooked or inaccessible by telephone, questionnaires were sent out. The number of replies was encouraging. However, those who replied tended to represent institutionalized groups with permanent staff. Some subcategories were harder to research than others. Business groups tend to be visible and accessible. In contrast, ethnic groups, although very numerous and active, are hard to contact because of frequent changes of address and because of a lack of permanent staff to answer enquiries.

While it was not possible to identify, let alone to contact, all the interest groups involved in the Canadian foreign policy making process, this survey begins the process by categorizing and discussing over 200 groups. Further studies are necessary to continue and expand upon the work begun in this paper.

ALPHABETICAL LISTING OF INTEREST GROUPS INVOLVED IN FOREIGN POLICY*

Air Industries Association of
    Canada
Suite 601, The Royal Trust Building
116 Albert Street
Ottawa, Ontario
KIP 5G3   tel: (613) 232-4297

Vice-President: Alex Bishop

Alberta Forest Products Association
Suite 204, 11710 Kingsway
    Avenue
Edmonton, Alberta
T5G 0X5   tel: (403) 452-2841

Manager: Arden Rytz

Alberta Wheat Pool (1923)
PO Box 2700, 505 Second Street
    West
Calgary, Alberta
T2P 2P5   tel: (403) 290-4910

Secretary: D.V. Riddell

Alpine Club of Canada
Box 1026
Banff, Alberta
TOL 0CO   tel: (403) 762-4481

Manager: Ron Matthews

*Information for this appendix was originally compiled in December 1982. To the extent possible, the information was brought up to date in July 1984.

Amnesty International Canada
(1973)
Suite 204, 294 Albert Street
Ottawa, Ontario
KIP 6E6   tel: (613) 563-1891

President: Robert Robertson

Amnistie internationale Canada
(1973)
Suite 400, 1800, boul Dorchester
ouest
Montréal, Québec
H3H 2H2   tél: (514) 931-5897/8

Président: Jean-Luc Hétu

Arab Palestine Association
PO Box 5165, Station A
Toronto, Ontario
M5W 1N5

President: Rashad Saleh

Association of Canadian
Community Colleges (1978)
110 Eglinton Avenue West
Toronto, Ontario
M4R 1A3   tel: (416) 489-5925

Director of Int Office: Suzanne
Hébert

Association of Canadian Financial
Corporations
115 Danforth Avenue
Toronto, Ontario
M4K 1N2   tel: (416) 461-9223

President: Carne Bray

Association of Canadian Television
and Radio Artists (ACTRA) (1963)
2239 Yonge Street
Toronto, Ontario
M4S 2B5   tel: (416) 489-1311

General Secretary: Paul Siren

Association of Consulting
Engineers of Canada
Suite 616, 130 Albert Street
Ottawa, Ontario
KIP 5G4   tel: (613) 236-0569

Managing Director: H.R. Pinault

L'Association des industries
forestières du Québec
Bureau 1300, 1155 Claire-Fontaine
Québec, Québec
GIR 3B2   tél: (418) 522-4027

Président et directeur général:
André Duchesne

84

Association québécoise des
organismes de coopération
internationale (1976)
1115, boul Gouin est
Montréal, Québec
H2C 1B3   tél: (514) 382-4560

Secrétaire permanent:
Jean Brodeur

Association of United Ukrainian
Canadians (1918)
962 Bloor Street West
Toronto, Ontario
M6H 1L6   tel: (416) 535-1063

*Secretary, National Executive
Committee*: W. Harasym

Atlantic Fisheries By-Products
Association (1941)
PO Box 991
Dartmouth, Nova Scotia
B2Y 3Z6   tel: (902) 463-7790

Atlantic Fishing Vessel Association
(1970)
PO Box 991
Dartmouth, Nova Scotia
B2Y 3Z6   tel. (902) 463-7790

Automotive Industries Association
of Canada
1272 Wellington Street
Ottawa, Ontario
K1Y 3A7   tel: (613) 728-5821

Executive Vice-President: Thomas
H. Whellams

Brazil-Canada Chamber of
Commerce
100 Adelaide Street West
Toronto, Ontario
M5H 1S3   tel: (416) 364-4634

General Manager: L.A. Bourgeois

Canada-Israel Chamber of
Commerce
PO Box 31
1 First Canadian Place
Toronto, Ontario
M5X 1A9   tel: (416) 362-7424

Executive Director: Nick Simmonds

Canada-Israel Committee (1973)
Suite 402, 980 Yonge Street
Toronto, Ontario
M4W 2J5   tel: (416) 924-0755

Director of Research: Shira Herzog
Besson

Canada-Japan Trade Council (1963)
Suite 903, 75 Albert Street
Ottawa, Ontario
KIP 5E7   tel: (613) 233-4047

President: N.G. Guthrie

Canada-USSR Association, Inc
(1950)
280 Queen Street West
Toronto, Ontario
M5V 2A1   tel: (416) 977-5819

Canadian Air Defence Officers
Association
250 Corot, Nun's Island
Montréal, Québec
H3E IK7   tel: (514) 877-7977

President: LCol A.M. Valenti, CD

Canadian Air Traffic Control
Association (1959)
Suite 604, 1 Nicholas Street
Ottawa, Ontario
KIN 7B7   tel: (613) 232-9413

President: W.J.Robertson

Canadian Air Line Pilots
Association (1937)
1300 Steeles Avenue East
Brampton, Ontario
L6T IA2   tel: (416) 453-8210

President: Capt R.E. Cook

Canadian Arctic Resources
Committee
Room 11, 46 Elgin Steet
Ottawa, Ontario
KIP 5K6   tel: (613) 236-7379

Executive Secretary: Kitson M.
Vincent

Canadian Association of Fish
Exporters (1978)
Suite 608, 77 Metcalfe Street
Ottawa, Ontario
KIP 5L6   tel: (613) 232-6325

President: R.W. Bulmer

Canadian Association – Latin
America and Caribbean
8th Floor, 42 Charles Street East
Toronto, Ontario
M4Y IT4   tel: (416) 964-6068

President: Marie Nicole Tempesta

Canadian Association of Young
Political Leaders
c/o Anne Scotton
#2, 554 Gilmour Street
Ottawa, Ontario
KIR 5L6   tel: (613) 994-1544

President: Anne Scotton

Canadian Bankers' Association
PO Box 282, Commercial Union
   Tower
Toronto-Dominion Centre
Toronto, Ontario
M5K 1K2   tel: (416) 362-6092

President: R.M. MacIntosh

Canadian Bar Association
Suite 1700, 130 Albert Street
Ottawa, Ontario
K1P 5G4   tel: (613) 237-2925

Executive Director: Bernard
   Blanchard

Canadian Business and Industry
   International Advisory
   Committee
151 Sparks Street
Ottawa, Ontario
K1P 5E3   tel: (613) 233-1845

Vice-Chairman: John Crean

Canadian Catholic Organization
   for Development and Peace
   (1967)
2111 Centre Street
Montréal, Québec
H3K 1J5   tel: (514) 932-5136

Executive Director: Jacques
   Champagne

Canadian Cattlemen's Association
4th Floor, 111 Sparks Street
Ottawa, Ontario
K1P 5B5   tel: (613) 233-9375

Canadian Chamber of Commerce
Suite 310, 200 Elgin Street
Ottawa, Ontario
K2P 2J7   tel: (613) 238-4000

President: S.F. Hughes

Canadian Chemical Producers'
   Association
Suite 805, 350 Sparks Street
Ottawa, Ontario
K1R 7S8   tel: (613) 237-6215

President: J.M. Bélanger

Canadian Coalition on Acid Rain
Suite 504, 112 St Clair Avenue
   West
Toronto, Ontario
M4V 2Y3   tel: (416) 968-2135

Executive Co-ordinator: Michael
   Perley

Canadian Committee of the Pacific
   Basin Economic Council
Suite 848, 99 Bank Street
Ottawa, Ontario
K1P 6B9   tel: (613) 238-6544

Director General: R. Lorne Seitz

Canadian Conference of Catholic
Bishops (1948)
90 Parent Avenue
Ottawa, Ontario
KIN 7B1   tel: (613) 236-9461

General Secretary: Rev D. Murphy

Canadian Council of Christians
and Jews
49 Front Street East
Toronto, Ontario
M5E 1B3   tel: (416) 364-3101

President and Chief Executive
Officer: Dr V. Goldbloom

Canadian Council of Churches
(1944)
40 St Clair Avenue East
Toronto, Ontario
M4T 1M9   tel: (416) 921-4152

General Secretary: Donald W.
Anderson

Canadian Council of the
International Chamber of
Commerce
Suite 1630, 1080 Beaver Hall Hill
Montréal, Québec
H2Z 1T2   tel: (514) 866-4334

President: B.G. Côté

Canadian Council for International
Co-operation (1968)
450 Rideau Street
Ottawa, Ontario
KIN 5Z4   tel: (613) 236-4547

Executive Director: Nigel Martin

Canadian Council of Professional
Engineers
Suite 401, 116 Albert Street
Ottawa, Ontario
KIP 5G3   tel: (613) 232-2474

Executive Director: Claude
Lajeunesse

The Canadian Education
Association (1891)
252 Bloor Street West
Toronto, Ontario
M5S 1V5   tel: (416) 924-7721

Executive Director: Dr F.K.
Stewart

Canadian Electrical Association
Suite 580, Westmount Square
Montréal, Québec
H3Z 2P9   tel: (514) 937-6181

General Manager: D.C. Campbell

Canadian Export Association
Suite 250, 99 Bank Street
Ottawa, Ontario
KIP 6B9   tel: (613) 238-8888

Chairman: J.H. Whalen

Canadian Federation of Agriculture
   (1935)
5th Floor, 111 Sparks Street
Ottawa, Ontario
KIP 5B5   tel: (613) 236-3633

Executive Secretary: David Kirk

Canadian Federation of Business
   and Professional Women's Clubs
Room 308, 56 Sparks Street
Ottawa, Ontario
KIP 5A9   tel: (613) 234-7619

President: Lucy Milne

Canadian Federation of Civil
   Liberties and Human Rights
   Association
323 Chapel Street
Ottawa, Ontario
KIN 7Z2   tel: (613) 235-8978
                              -2667

President: Dr Don Whiteside

Canadian Federation of Labour
   (1982)
Suite 300, 107 Sparks Street
Ottawa, Ontario
KIP 5E3   tel: (613) 234-4141

President: James McCambly

Canadian Federation of Students
Suite 202, 126 York Street
Ottawa, Ontario
KIN 5T5   tel: (613) 232-7394

Canadian Forces Communication
   and Electronics Association
2316 Hillary Avenue
Ottawa, Ontario
KIH 7J3   tel: (613) 996-7844

President: BGen M.H.F. Webber,
CD

Canadian Forces Logistics
   Association
15 Birchwood Drive
Armsdale
Halifax, Nova Scotia
B3N 1H7   tel: (902) 477-3428

President: LCol J. West, CD

Canadian Forestry Association
(1900)
Suite 203, 185 Somerset Street
West
Ottawa, Ontario
K2P OJ2   tel: (613) 232-1815

Executive Director: A.D. Hall, RPF

The Canadian Friends Service
Committee (1931)
60 Lowther Avenue
Toronto, Ontario
M5R IC7   tel: (416) 920-5213

Executive Secretary: Mrs Ruth
Morris

Canadian Horticultural Council
(1922)
3 Amberwood Crescent
Nepean, Ontario
K2E 7LI   tel: (613) 226-4187

Executive Vice-President: William
Daman

Canadian Hunger Foundation
323 Chapel Street
Ottawa, Ontario
KIN 7Z2   tel: (613) 237-0180

Executive Director: John Laidlaw

Canadian Importers Association
60 Harbour Street
Toronto, Ontario
M5J IB7   tel: (416) 862-0002

President: Keith G. Dixon

Canadian Infantry Association
(1912)
6607 Law Drive SW
Calgary, Alberta
T3E 6A2   tel: (403) 268-5108

President: Col S.E. Blakely, CD

Canadian Institute of International
Affairs (1928)
15 King's College Circle
Toronto, Ontario
M5S 2V9   tel: (416) 979-1851

Executive Director: Jacques
Rastoul

Canadian Institute of Mining and
Metallurgy (1898)
Suite 400, 1130 Sherbrooke Street
West
Montréal, Québec
H3A 2M8   tel: (514) 842-3461

Executive Director: Pierre Michaud

Canadian Institute of Strategic
  Studies
185 Bloor Street East
Toronto, Ontario
M4W IEI   tel: (416) 964-2872

Executive Director: LCol Brian S.
  MacDonald

Canadian Intelligence & Security
  Association
42 Kidgrove Gardens
Nepean, Ontario
K2G 3W6   tel: (819) 997-5132

President: Col R.T. Grogan, CD

Canadian Jewish Congress
1590, avenue Docteur Penfield
Montréal, Québec
H3G IC5   tel: (514) 931-7531

Executive Director: Alan Rese

Canadian Labour Congress (1956)
2841 Riverside Drive
Ottawa, Ontario
KIV 8X7   tel: (613) 521-3400

President: Dennis McDermott

Canadian League for the
  Liberation of the Ukraine (1950)
140 Bathurst Street
Toronto, Ontario
M5V 2R3   tel: (416) 366-9350

Canadian Lumbermen's Association
27 Goulburn Avenue
Ottawa, Ontario
KIN 8C7   tel: (613) 233-6205

Executive Director: Jack
  McCracken

Canadian Lutheran World Relief
  (1946)
1820 Arlington Street
Winnipeg, Manitoba
R2X IW4   tel: (204) 586-8558

Executive Director: J.G. Keil

Canadian Manufacturers'
  Association
Suite 1400, 1 Yonge Street
Toronto, Ontario
M5E IJ9   tel: (416) 363-7261

Executive Director: Roy A.
  Phillips

Canadian Maritime Law Association
620 St James Street
Montréal, Québec
H3C IC7   tel: (514) 849-4201

Honorary Secretary: W.T. Smith

Canadian Nature Federation (1971)
Suite 203, 75 Albert Street
Ottawa, Ontario
KIP 6GI   tel: (613) 238-6154

Environmental Director: Greg
  Sheehy

Canadian Nuclear Association
11th Floor, 111 Elizabeth Street
Toronto, Ontario
M5G 1P7   tel: (416) 977-6152

President: Dr Norman Aspen

Canadian Nuclear Society
11th Floor, 111 Elizabeth Street
Toronto, Ontario
M5G 1P7   tel: (416) 977-6152

President: P. Ross-Ross

Canadian Peace Congress (1948)
Rooms 301–302, 671 Danforth Ave.
Toronto, Ontario
M4J 1L3   tel: (416) 469-3422

Executive Director: Gordon
  Flowers

Canadian Petroleum Association
  (1952)
Suite 1500, 633 6th Avenue SW
Calgary, Alberta
T2P 2Y5   tel: (403) 269-6721

Executive Director: Ian R. Smyth

Canadian Polish Congress (1944)
288 Roncesvalles Avenue
Toronto, Ontario
M6R 2M4   tel: (416) 532-2876

President: J. Kaszuba

Canadian Pork Council (1966)
111 Sparks Street
Ottawa, Ontario
KIP 5B5   tel: (613) 236-3633

Secretary Treasurer: William
  Hamilton

Canadian Professors for Peace in
  the Middle East
491 Lawrence Avenue West
Toronto, Ontario
M5M 1C7   tel: (416) 789-3495

Canadian Pugwash Group
c/o Mr W. Epstein
15 King's College Circle
Toronto, Ontario
M5S 2V9

Chairman: William Epstein

Canadian Pulp and Paper
  Association (1913)
Suite 2300, 1155 Metcalfe Street
Montréal, Québec
H3B 2X9   tel: (514) 866-6621

President: Howard Hart

Canadian Save the Children Fund
720 Spadina Avenue
Toronto, Ontario
M5S 2W3   tel: (416) 960-3190

National Director: Gordon S.
  Ramsay

Canadian Study Group on Arms
  Control and Disarmament
c/o 15 King's College Circle
Toronto, Ontario
M5S 2V9   tel: (416) 979-1851

Co-convenors: John Lamb
                Robert Reford

Canadian Textile Importers
  Association
Suite 511, 99 Chabanel Street West
Montréal, Québec
H2N 1C3   tel: (514) 381-8569

Canadian Textiles Institute (1935)
Suite 1002, 1080 Beaver Hall Hill
Montréal, Québec
H2Z 1T6   tel: (514) 866-2081

President: E.L. Barry

Canadian Trucking Association
  (1939)
Suite 300, 130 Albert Street
Ottawa, Ontario
K1P 5G4   tel: (613) 236-9426

Executive Director: A.K. Maclaren

Canadian Wildlife Federation
  (1961)
1673 Carling Avenue
Ottawa, Ontario
K2A 1C4   tel: (613) 725-2191

Canadian Wood Council
85 Albert Street
Ottawa, Ontario
K1P 6A4   tel: (613) 235-7221

Executive Vice-President: Robert
  F. DeGrace

Central Forest Products Association
14G, 1975 Corydon Avenue
Winnipeg, Manitoba
R3P 0R1   tel: (204) 489-5749

Secretary Manager: A. Stuesser

Centre des services sociaux
    Montréal métropolitain
879, rue Sherbrooke est
Montréal, Québec
H2L 1K9

Waheed Malik

Centre for Spanish Speaking
  People
582-A College Street
Toronto, Ontario
M6G 1B3   tel: (416) 533-8545

Frank Luce

Children's Apparel Manufacturers
Association
Suite 304, 8235 Mountain Sights
Avenue
Montréal, Québec
H4P 2B4   tel: (514) 731-7774

Christian Movement for Peace
(1969)
427 Bloor Street West
Toronto, Ontario
M5S 1X7   tel: (416) 921-2360

Ms J. Huntley

Citizens for Public Justice (1963)
3rd Floor, 229 College street
Toronto, Ontario
M5T 1R4   tel: (416) 979-2443

Coalition for World Disarmament
(1977)
1414 West 12th Avenue
Vancouver, British Columbia
V6H 1M8   tel: (604) 731-5626

Committee for an Independent
Canada
Suite 48, 46 Elgin Street
Ottawa, Ontario
K1P 5K6   tel: (613) 238-2730

Executive Director: Daryl Logan

Confectionery Manufacturers
Association
Suite 101, 1185 Eglinton Avenue
East
Toronto, Ontario
M3C 3C6   tel: (416) 429-1046

General Manager: Philip Moyes

Confederation of Church and
Business People
15 Wellington Street West
Toronto, Ontario
M5J 1G7   tel: (416) 366-1583

General Manager: Grant Lennie

Confederation of National Trade
Unions (1921)
1601, rue Delorimier
Montréal, Québec
H2K 2M4   tel: (514) 598-2121

General President: Norbert
Rodrique

Conference Board of Canada
(1954)
25 McArthur Avenue
Ottawa, Ontario
K1L 6R3   tel: (613) 746-1261

President: James R. Nininger

Conference of Defence Associations
(1932)
PO Box 893
Ottawa, Ontario
KIP 5P9   tel: (613) 995-8599

Chairman: LCol H.A.J.
Hutchinson

Conservation Council of New
Brunswick
180 St John Street
Fredericton, New Brunswick
E3B 4A9   tel: (506) 454-6062

The Conservation Council of
Ontario (1952)
6th Floor, 45 Charles Street East
Toronto, Ontario
M4Y 1S2   tel: (416) 961-6830

Executive Director: Dr Arthur M.
Timms

Consulting Engineers of Ontario
86 Overlea Boulevard
Toronto, Ontario
M4H 1C6   tel: (416) 425-8027

Executive Director: Ross F. Reid

Consumers' Association of Canada
(1947)
2660 Southvale Crescent – Level 3
Ottawa, Ontario
KIB 5C4   tel: (613) 733-9450

President: Mrs Barbara Shand

Co-operative Development
Foundation of Canada
237 Metcalfe Street
Ottawa, Ontario
K2P 1R2   tel: (613) 238-6711

*Director of International Develop-
ment*: Lorraine Messier Hubbert

Council of Forest Industries of
British Columbia
Suite 1500, Guinness Towers
1055 West Hastings Street
Vancouver, British Columbia
V6E 2H1   tel: (604) 684-0211

*President and Chief Executive
Officer*: D.A.S. Lanskail

Croatian Canadian Association
1621 Dupont Street
Toronto, Ontario
M6P 3S8   tel: (416) 537-4749

N.R. Halls

CUSO
151 Slater Street
Ottawa, Ontario
KIP 5H5   tel: (613) 563-1242

Executive Director: Chris Bryant

Czechoslovak National Association
    of Canada
740 Spadina Avenue
Toronto, Ontario
M5S 2J2   tel: (416) 925-2241

Dairy Farmers of Canada (1934)
111 Sparks Street
Ottawa, Ontario
KIP 5B5   tel: (613) 236-9997

Defence Medical Association of
    Canada
73 Culliton Crescent
Regina, Saskatchewan
S4S 4J5   tel: (306) 586-5341

President: LCol W.B. MacDonald,
    CD

Ducks Unlimited (Canada) (1937)
1190 Waverley Street
Winnipeg, Manitoba
R3T 2E2   tel: (204) 477-1760

Executive Vice-President: D.
    Stewart Morrison

Ecumenical Forum of Canada
11 Madison Avenue
Toronto, Ontario
M5R 2S2   tel: (416) 924-9351

Director: Michael Cooke

Energy and Chemical Workers
    Union (1980)
#44, 9912 – 106 Street
Edmonton, Alberta
T5K 1C5   tel: (403) 422-7932

National Director: C. Neil Reimer

Energy Probe (1971)
100 College Street
Toronto, Ontario
M5G 1L5   tel: (416) 978-7014

Fédération canadienne des
    travailleurs du textile inc
    (1936)
Suite 600, 1259, rue Berri
Montréal, Québec
H2L 4C7   tél: (514) 842-6941

Président: Armand Gagnon

Federation of Italian-Canadian
    Associations and Clubs (1970)
756 Ossington Avenue
Toronto, Ontario
M6G 3T9   tel: (416) 531-9964

Fisheries Association of British
Columbia
Room 400, 100 West Pender Street
Vancouver, British Columbia
V6B 1R8   tel: (604) 684-6454

Fisheries Association of Newfound-
land and Labrador Ltd (1944)
PO Box 8900
10 O'Leary Avenue
St John's, Newfoundland
A1B 3R9   tel: (709) 726-7223

President: W.E. Wells

Fisheries Council of Canada (1945)
Suite 603, 77 Metcalfe Street
Ottawa, Ontario
K1P 5L6   tel: (613) 238-7751

President: Kenneth M. Campbell

Friends of the Earth – Canada
(1978)
Suite 53, 53 Queen Street
Ottawa, Ontario
K1P 5C5   tel: (613) 235-3860

Executive Director: Ray Bles

Great Lakes Tomorrow (1975)
c/o Conservation Council of
Ontario
5th Floor, 45 Charles Street East
Toronto, Ontario
M4Y 1S2   tel: (416) 961-6830

Greek Canadian Democratic
Organization
290 Danforth Avenue
Toronto, Ontario
M4K 1N6   tel: (416) 461-7300

Greenpeace Foundation (Canada)
(1970)
2623 West Fourth Avenue
Vancouver, British Columbia
V6K 1P8   tel: (604) 736-0321

President: Dr Pat Moore

Hungarian Canadian Federation
840 St Clair Avenue West
Toronto, Ontario
M6C 1C1   tel: (416) 654-4926

Imperial Order Daughters of the
Empire (1917)
Suite 254, 40 Orchard View Blvd
Toronto, Ontario
M4R 1B9   tel: (416) 487-4416

National Secretary: Mrs J.W.
Houston

Inter Pares (1975)
205 Pretoria Avenue
Ottawa, Ontario
K1S 1X1   tel: (613) 563-4801

Director: Tim Brodhead

Intercede
348 College Street
Toronto, Ontario
M5T 1S4   tel: (416) 929-3240

Inter-Church Committee for
  Refugees
Suite 201, 40 St Clair Avenue East
Toronto, Ontario
M4T 1M9   tel: (416) 921-4152

Chairman: Bernard Daly

Inter-Church Fund for International
  Development
Suite 314, 85 St Clair Avenue East
Toronto, Ontario
M4T 1M8   tel: (416) 968-1411

Bob Fugere

The International Atlantic Salmon
  Foundation (1968)
PO Box 429
St Andrews, New Brunswick
E0G 2X0   tel: (506) 529-8818

Executive Director: Dr Wilfred
  M. Carter

International Defence and Aid
  Fund for Southern Africa
  (Canada) (1980)
78 Daly Avenue
Ottawa, Ontario
K1P 5R1   tel: (613) 233-5939

Executive Secretary: Anne Mitchell

International Development Office
  (1978)
Association of Universities and
  Colleges of Canada
151 Slater Street
Ottawa, Ontario
K1P 5N1   tel: (613) 563-1236

Executive Director: Dr A.K.
  Gilmour

International Labour Organization,
  Canada Branch
#202, 75 Albert Street
Ottawa, Ontario
K1P 5E7   tel: (613) 233-1114

Director: J.R.W. Whitehouse

Jamaican Canadian Association
Box 532, Terminal A
Toronto, Ontario
M5W 1E4   tel: (416) 789-0623

Judicial Action Agenda (1980)
Suite 202, 5600 Dalhousie Road
Vancouver, British Columbia
v6t 1w4   tel: (604) 224-0803

Land Ordnance Engineering
    Branch Association
11108 – 36 A Avenue
Edmonton, Alberta
t6j 0e5   tel: (403) 428-9597

President: Maj D.E. Hillman, CD

Latvian National Federation in
    Canada
491 College Street
Toronto, Ontario
m6g 1a5   tel: (416) 922-5418

Maison de l'Amitié
120, avenue Duluth est
Montréal, Québec
h2w 1s1   tél: (514) 843-4356

Juan Iturriaga

Manitoba Council for International
    Co-operation
418 Wardlaw Avenue
Winnipeg, Manitoba
r3l 0l7   tel: (204) 475-4169

Executive Director: Mary Stuart

Maritime Defence Association of
    Canada
975 Linkleas Avenue
Victoria, British Columbia
v8s 5c4   tel: (604) 598-4880

President: Capt (N) M.L. Hadley,
    CD

Maritime Lumber Bureau (1938)
Box 459
Amherst, Nova Scotia
b4h 4a1   tel: (902) 667-3889

Executive Director: A.G. (Tony)
    Rumbold

Match International Centre
Suite 401, 171 Nepean Street
Ottawa, Ontario
k2p 0b5   tel: (613) 238-1312

Executive Director: Sara Camblin-
    Breault

Mennonite Central Committee
    (Canada)
1483 Pembina Highway (201)
Winnipeg, Manitoba
r3t 2c8   tel: (204) 475-3550

Executive Secretary: J.M. Klassen

Middle East Discussion Group
(1981)
c/o M.-N. Choquet
421 Laurier Avenue East
Ottawa, Ontario
KIN 6R4   tel: (613) 563-0016

Marie-N. Choquet

Military Engineers Association of
Canada
54 Banting Way
Kanata, Ontario
K2K 1P8   tel: (613) 998-8032

President: Maj R.E.R. Stanfield,
CD

Mining Association of Canada
(1935)
Suite 705, 350 Sparks Street
Ottawa, Ontario
KIR 7S8   tel: (613) 233-9391

Managing Director: John L. Bonus

Mission catholique latino-
americaine
805, rue Villeray
Montréal, Québec
H2R 1J4

Raul Garcia Zavala

National Action Committee on the
Status of Women (1966)
Suite 306, 40 St Clair Avenue East
Toronto, Ontario
M4T 1M9   tel: (416) 922-3246

President: Chaviva Hosek

National Citizens Coalition
Suite 907, 100 Adelaide Street West
Toronto, Ontario
M5H 1S3   tel: (416) 869-3838

President: Colin Brown

National Council of YMCAS of
Canada (1851)
2160 Yonge Street
Toronto, Ontario
M4S 2A9   tel: (416) 485-9447

National General Secretary:
Rix Rogers

National Dairy Council of Canada
Suite 704, 141 Laurier Avenue West
Ottawa, Ontario
KIP 5J3   tel: (613) 238-4116

President: Kempton L. Matte

National Farmers Union (1969)
250-C 2nd Avenue South
Saskatoon, Saskatchewan
S7K 2M1   tel: (306) 652-9465

President: Ted Strain

National and Provincial Parks
Association of Canada
Suite 308, 47 Colborne Street
Toronto, Ontario
M5E 1E3   tel: (416) 366-3494

National Survival Institute (1973)
3rd Floor, 229 College Street
Toronto, Ontario
M5T 1R4   tel: (416) 593-1299

Executive Director: Bea Olivastri

Naval Officers Association of
Canada
1107 Avenue Road
Toronto, Ontario
M5N 2E4   tel: (416) 481-3319

Secretary: Frank C. Manchee

Navy League of Canada (1895)
4 Queen Elizabeth Drive
Ottawa, Ontario
K2P 2H9   tel: (613) 232-2784

General Manager: W.J. Hodge

New Brunswick Forest Products
Association
500 Beaverbrook Court
Fredericton, New Brunswick
E3B 5X4   tel: (506) 455-0998

Executive Director: Don Lockhart

North-South Institute
185 Rideau Street
Ottawa, Ontario
KIN 5X8   tel: (613) 236-3535

Executive Director: Bernard Wood

Nova Scotia Forest Products
Association (1934)
300 Mill Street
Box 696
Truro, Nova Scotia
B2N 5E5   tel: (902) 895-1179

Executive Director: Lorne E. Etter

Ontario Forest Industries
Association
Suite 1700, 130 Adelaide Street
West
Toronto, Ontario
M5H 3P5   tel: (416) 368-6188

President: Ken Greaves

Ontario Forestry Association
Room 209, 150 Consumers Road
Willowdale, Ontario
M2J 1P9   tel: (416) 493-4565

Ontario Lumber Manufacturers'
Association
Suite 414, 159 Bay Street
Toronto, Ontario
M5J 1J7   tel: (416) 367-9717

Executive Director: Art Herridge

Operation Dismantle
Box 3887, Station C
Ottawa, Ontario
KIY IT9   tel: (613) 722-6001

Director: James Stark

Operation Life Line
8 York Street
Toronto, Ontario
M5J IR2   tel: (416) 363-0211

Organization of CANDU Industries
c/o J.M. Douglas
1 Yonge Street
Toronto, Ontario
M5E IJ9   tel: (416) 363-7261

Secretary and General Manager:
    J.M. Douglas

Oxfam Canada (1966)
Suite 301, 251 Laurier Avenue
    West
Ottawa, Ontario
KIP 5J6   tel: (613) 237-5236

National Secretary: Lawrence
    Cumming

Oxfam-Québec
169 est, rue St-Paul
Montréal, Québec
H2Y IG8   tél: (514) 866-1773

Directeur général: Jean Loiselle

Palliser Wheat Growers Association
    (1970)
201 – 4401 Albert Street
Regina, Saskatchewan
S4S 6B6   tel: (306) 586-5866

Executive Director: Don Baron

Physicians for Social Responsibility
Suite 406, 360 Bloor Street West
Toronto, Ontario
M5S IXI   tel: (416) 922-7335

Dr F.G. Sommers

Polish Democratic Association
2094 Dundas Street West
Toronto, Ontario
M6R IW9   tel: (416) 535-3295

Pollution Probe (1969, incorp.
    1971)
12 Madison Avenue
Toronto, Ontario
M5R 2SI   tel: (416) 978-6155
                                -7152

Executive Director: Colin F.W.
    Isaacs

Pollution Probe (Ottawa-Carleton)
53 Queen Street
Ottawa, Ontario
KIP 5C5   tel: (613) 235-9266

Portuguese Association of Canada
4170 St Urbain Street
Montréal, Québec
H2W 1V3   tel: (514) 844-2269

Presbyterian Church in Canada
   (1875)
50 Wynford Drive
Don Mills, Ontario
M3C 1J7   tel: (416) 441-1111

Administrative Assistant: Jean
   Davidson

Primate's World Relief and
   Development Fund
Anglican Church of Canada
   (1959)
600 Jarvis Street
Toronto, Ontario
M4Y 2J6   tel: (416) 924-9192

General Secretary: George H.
   Cram

Project Ploughshares (1976)
321 Chapel Street
Ottawa, Ontario
K1N 7Z2   tel: (613) 236-4547

Chairman of the Board: Dr Clarke
   MacDonald

Prospectors and Developers
   Association (1932)
Suite 219, 159 Bay Street
Toronto, Ontario
M5J 1J7   tel: (416) 362-1969

General Manager: J. William
   Griffith

Public Focus on Great Lakes
   Pollution
894 Manning Avenue
Toronto, Ontario
M6G 2X4   tel: (416) 533-3508

Retail Council of Canada
Suite 212, 214 King Street West
Toronto, Ontario
M5H 1K4   tel: (416) 598-4684

President: Alasdair McKichan

Retail Merchants Association of
   Canada (1896)
1780 Birchmount Road
Scarborough, Ontario
M1P 2H8   tel: (416) 291-7903

General Manager: George E.
   Crompton

Royal Canadian Air Force
Association (1948)
424 Metcalfe Street
Ottawa, Ontario
K2P 2C3   tel: (613) 236-1074

General Manager: Len Lapeer

Royal Canadian Armoured Corps
Association
400 University Avenue
Toronto, Ontario
M5G 1S7   tel: (416) 595-7319

President: LCol G.I. Mathieson,
CD

Royal Canadian Artillery
Association
15 Rusholme Crescent
St Catharines, Ontario
L2T 3V3   tel: (416) 682-2397

President: BGen L.M. Salmon, CD

Royal Canadian Dental Corps
Association
26 Southdale Drive
Markham, Ontario
L3P 1J7   tel: (416) 294-1294

President: Maj C.G. Hunt, CD

Saskatchewan Council for Inter-
national Co-operation (1974)
Huston House
2138 McIntyre Street
Regina, Saskatchewan
S4P 2R7   tel: (306) 527-4669

Co-executive Secretary:
Lynn Fogwill/Gerry Sutton

Saskatchewan Wheat Pool
Wheat Pool Building
2625 Victoria Avenue
Regina, Saskatchewan
S4T 7T9   tel: (306) 569-4411

Secretary: J.O. Wright

Science for Peace (1981)
c/o University College
University of Toronto
Toronto, Ontario
M5S 1A1   tel: (416) 978-6930

President: Anatol Rapoport

Seafood Producers Association of
Nova Scotia (SPANS) (1944)
PO Box 991
Dartmouth, Nova Scotia
B2Y 3Z6   tel: (902) 463-7790

Executive Director: R.C. Stirling

Service universitaire canadien
   outre-mer (1961)
4824 Côte-des-Neiges
Montréal, Québec
H3V 1G4   tél: (514) 735-4561

Directeur exécutif: Yvon Madore

Services communautaires catho-
   liques
1857, boul de Maisonneuve ouest
Montréal, Québec
H3H 1J9   tél: (514) 937-5351

Mme Thérèse Jubinville

The Shipping Federation of
   Canada (1903)
Room 326, 300 St Sacrement
   Street
Montréal, Québec
H2Y 1X4   tel: (514) 849-2325

President: J.A. Crichton

Shoe Manufacturers' Association
   of Canada (1918)
Suite 710, 1010 St Catherine St W
Montréal, Québec
H3B 3R4   tel: (514) 878-9337

President: Jean-Guy Maheu, CA

The Sierra Club
1200 Hornby Street
Vancouver, British Columbia
V6Z 2E2   tel: (604) 687-3333

Sierra Club of Western Canada
Box 202
Victoria, British Columbia
V8W 2M6

Director: R. Nixon

Southern Africa Action Coalition
2524 Cypress Street
Vancouver, British Columbia
V6J 3N2   tel: (604) 734-1712

Secretary: Karensa Lai

SPEC
Vancouver Central Office
2150 Maple Street
Vancouver, British Columbia
V6J 3T3   tel: (604) 736-5601

STOP (Save Tomorrow, Oppose
   Pollution)
10523 77th Avenue
Edmonton, Alberta
T5J 2N9   tel: (403) 432-7926

Swiss Canadian Chamber of
   Commerce (Montréal) Inc
   (1971)
1572 Dr Penfield Avenue
Montréal, Québec
H3G 1C4   tel: (514) 937-5822

President: Peter Schibler

Swiss Canadian Chamber of
Commerce (Toronto) Inc
21 Iron Street
Rexdale, Ontario
M9W 5E3   tel: (416) 243-1201

President: William Mawhinney

Taskforce on Churches and
Corporate Responsibility
129 St Clair Avenue West
Toronto, Ontario
M4V 1N5   tel: (416) 923-1758

Co-ordinator: Renate Pratt

Textile Trade Association (1931)
Room 1059, 1435 St Alexander
Street
Montréal, Québec
H3A 2G4   tel: (514) 842-1497

Executive Director: I.L. Goldner

Toronto Committee for the
Liberation of Southern Africa
121 Avenue Road
Toronto, Ontario
M5R 2G3   tel: (416) 967-5562

Co-ordinator: Carole Houlihan

Ukrainian National Federation
2397-A Bloor Street West
Toronto, Ontario
M6S 4T2   tel: (416) 767-1248

President: Mr Mastykask

UNHCR Branch Office Ottawa
Suite 401, 280 Albert Street
Ottawa, Ontario
K1P 5G8   tel: (613) 232-0909

Unicef Canada
443 Mt Pleasant Road
Toronto, Ontario
M4S 2L8   tel: (416) 482-4444

Unifarm (1970)
14815 119 Avenue
Edmonton, Alberta
T5L 2N8   tel: (403) 451-5912

Executive Secretary: W.J. Plosz

United Automobile Workers of
America
205 Placer Crt
Toronto, Ontario
M2H 3H9   tel: (416) 497-4110

United Church of Canada (1925)
85 St Clair Avenue East
Toronto, Ontario
M4T 1M8   tel: (416) 925-5931

Development Secretary: Glenna
  Graham

United Jewish Peoples Order,
  Jewish Assistance and Social
  Organization Inc
3737 Van Horne Avenue
Montréal, Québec
H3S 1R9   tel: (514) 735-2878

President: Norman Massy

United Nations Association in
  Canada (1946)
Suite 808, 63 Sparks Street
Ottawa, Ontario
K1P 5A6   tel: (613) 232-5751

Executive Director: Firdaus
  Kharas

United Steelworkers of America
  (1936)
234 Eglinton Avenue East, 7th
  Floor
Toronto, Ontario
M4P 1K7   tel: (416) 487-1571

Voice of Women
175 Carlton Street
Toronto, Ontario
M5A 2K3   tel: (416) 922-2997

National Coordinator: Dorothy
  Smieciuck

Women's International League for
  Peace and Freedom (1915)
Box 4781, Station E
Ottawa, Ontario
K1S 5H9   tel: (613) 232-6382

Workers Benevolent Association
  (1922)
595 Pritchard Avenue
Winnipeg, Manitoba
R2W 2K4   tel: (204) 589-4397

National Secretary: Zenovy
  Nykolyshyn, RSW

World Conference on Religion for
  Peace (Canada) (1976)
11 Madison Avenue
Toronto, Ontario
M5R 2S2   tel: (416) 924-9351

National President: Fredelle Brief

World Federalists of Canada
(1965)
Suite 32, 46 Elgin Street
Ottawa, Ontario
KIP 5K6   tel: (613) 232-0647

President: Dr Hanna Newcombe

World University Service of
Canada (1939)
Box 3000, Station C
Ottawa, Ontario
KIY 4M8   tel: (613) 725-3121

Executive Director: William W.
McNeill

World Vision Canada (1959)
6630 Turner Valley Road
Mississauga, Ontario
L5N 2S4   tel: (416) 821-3030

Executive Director: Rev William J.
Newell

YMCA de Montréal
1441, rue Drummond
Montréal, Québec
H3G 1W3   tél: (514) 849-5331

Directeur: Solomon Kasimer

APPENDIX C
LIST OF INTERVIEWEES

PAT ADAMS, Research Assistant, Energy Probe: 11 March 1982

DIANE ADSHEAD, Office Manager, Match International Centre: 26 May 1982

T. ANDERSON, International Division, Canadian Bankers' Association: 17 March 1982

THOMAS ANTHONY, Director, World Progress, Anglican Church of Canada: 5 May 1982

NORMAN ASPEN, President, Canadian Nuclear Association: 9 March 1982

E.L. BARRY, President, Canadian Textiles Institute: 20 May 1982

MARGARET BIGGS, North-South Institute: 31 March 1982

ALEX BISHOP, Vice-President, Air Industries Association of Canada: 26 March 1982

FRANÇOISE BLANCHARD, Secretary to the President, Canadian Pulp and Paper Association: 26 May 1982

JOHN L. BONUS, Managing Director, Mining Association of Canada: 20 May 1982

L.A. BOURGEOIS, General Manager, Brazil-Canada Chamber of Commerce: 5 May 1982

MARGARET BOYCE, Representative, Voice of Women: 18 May 1982

FREDELLE BRIEF, National President, World Conference on Religion for Peace (Canada): 18 May 1982

ELISE BRIERE, Canadian Bar Association: 26 May 1982

TIM BRODHEAD, Director, Inter Pares: 20 May 1982

K.C. BROWN, Chairman, Refugee Status Advisory Committee, Department of Employment and Immigration: 1 April 1982

WILLIAM G. BROWNE, Manager, Canadian Chamber of Commerce: 20 May 1982

JENNIFER BROWNELL, Representative, Canadian Save the Children Fund

JEAN CAMPBELL, Representative, Ecumenical Forum: 17 February 1982

BRUCE CHAPMAN, Director of Industrial Operations, Fisheries Council of Canada: 20 May 1982

PATRICIA CLOSE, Department of Energy, Mines and Resources: 31 March 1982

GENEVIEVE COWGILL, Representative, Amnesty International: 10 March 1982.

JOHN CREAN, Vice-Chairman, Canadian Business and Industry International Committee: 12 February 1982

STUART CULBERTSON, Director of Trade Research, Canadian Importers Association Inc: 15 March 1982

BERNARD DALY, Member of the Pastoral Team for Research and Planning, Canadian Conference of Catholic Bishops: 20 May 1982

ALBERT DESCHAMPS, Ottawa Representative, Canadian Manufacturers' Association: 7 April 1982

PETER DOBELL, Director, Parliamentary Centre for Foreign Affairs and Foreign Trade: 31 March 1982

PEARL DOBSON, Executive Secretary, National Council of Women: 26 May 1982

DEBRA DOUGLAS, Editor, Canadian Export Association: 20 May 1982

JACQUELINE DUBUC, Secretary to the President, Confederation of National Trade Unions: 20 May 1982

JOAN DUERR, Canadian Friends Service Committee: 17 March 1982

ERIC FAWCETT, Representative, Science for Peace: 18 May 1982

GLENN FLATEN, President, Canadian Federation of Agriculture: 20 May 1982

GORDON FLOWERS, Executive Director, Canadian Peace Congress: 11 March 1982

MARION FULLER, Consumers' Association of Canada: 20 May 1982

BILL GALBRAITH, Information Specialist, Conference Board of Canada: 20 May 1982

A. GERTLER, Representative, Voice of Women: 2 April 1982

BARBARA GIBAULT, Co-operation for Development Consultant, YWCA of Canada: 18 May 1982

DOUG GLYNN, Public Relations Department, United Automobile Workers of America: 11 March 1982

V. GOLDBLOOM, President and Chief Executive Officer, Canadian Council of Christians and Jews: 14 March 1982

I.L. GOLDNER, Executive Director, Textile Trade Association: 20 May 1982

L.J. GORDON, Public Affairs Director, Information Directorate, Department of Environment: 5 April 1982

BONNIE GREEN, Secretary to the Committee on Church and International Affairs, United Church of Canada: 25 May 1982

N.G. GUTHRIE, President, Canada-Japan Trade Council: 20 May 1982

A.D. HALL, RPF, Executive Director, Canadian Forestry Association: 20 May 1982

CAROL HALL, United Nations Association in Canada: 18 March 1982

MACKIE HALL, Assistant to the Director General, Canadian Committee of the Pacific Basin Economic Council: 26 May 1982

DOROTHY HANSEN, Friends of the Earth (Canada): 20 May 1982

H. JOHN HARKER, Director, International Affairs Department, Canadian Labour Congress: 7 April 1982

RICHARD HARMSTON, Executive Director, Canadian Council for International Co-operation: 5 April 1982

SUZANNE HÉBERT, Director of International Office, Association of Canadian Community Colleges: 19 April 1982

PEGGY HEPPES, Managing Director, Canadian Nature Federation: 20 May 1982

MAXINE HERMOLIN, Representative, National Action Committee on the Status of Women: 26 May 1982

SHIRA HERZOG BESSIN, Director of Research, Canada-Israel Committee: 11 March 1982

B. HEXTER, Administrative Co-ordinator to C.T. Charland, Assistant Deputy Minister, Trade Development, Department of External Affairs: 30 March 1982

JULIET HUNTLY, Representative, Christian Movement for Peace: 18 March 1982

COLIN F.W. ISAACS, Executive Director, Pollution Probe: 22 December 1982

WILLIAM JANZEN, Director, Mennonite Central Committee (Canada): 6 April 1982

W.J. JENKINS, Assistant Deputy Minister, Sectoral and Economic Relations, Department of External Affairs: 26 March 1982

WARREN JOHANNSON, International Policy (Air), Transport Canada: 6 April 1982

J. KASZUBA, President, Canadian Polish Congress: 18 May 1982

H. KROLL, Southern Africa, African Affairs (Anglophone) Division, Department of External Affairs: 31 March 1982

JOHN LAMB, Co-convenor, Canadian Study Group on Arms Control and Disarmament: 14 April 1982

R.E. LATIMER, Assistant Deputy Minister, Area Trade Relations, Department of External Affairs: 26 March 1982

H.A. LAWLESS, Director, Domestic Information Programs Division, Department of External Affairs: 30 March 1982

J.C. LEGG, Deputy Director, Arms Control and Disarmament Division, Department of External Affairs: 31 March 1982

GRANT LENNIE, General Manager, Confederation of Church and Business People: 18 May 1982

CHRISTINE LUNDY, Projects Officer, Unicef Canada: 18 March 1982

DOMINIQUE LUPIEN, Canadian Council of Professional Engineers: 26 May 1982

PEYTON LYON, School of International Affairs, Carleton University: 26 March 1982

BRIAN MACDONALD, Executive Director, Canadian Institute of Strategic Studies: 20 April 1982

CLARKE MACDONALD, United Church of Canada: 11 May 1982

K.W. MACLELLAN, Director General, Office of Internal Evaluation and Audit, Department of External Affairs: 26 March 1982

J.A. MACPHERSON, Director General, Bureau of Economic Intelligence, Department of External Affairs: 29 March 1982

MAUREEN MOLOT, Associate Director, Department of Political Science, Carleton University: 1 April 1982

FRANK C. MANCHEE, Past National President, Naval Officers Association of Canada: 17 March 1982

LYNNE C. MARTIN, Project Co-ordinator, *Peace Unearth: A Directory of Canadian Peace Organizations with International Concerns:* 21 May 1982

WILLIAM MAWHINNEY, President, Swiss Canadian Chamber of Commerce (Toronto) Inc: 18 May 1982

A.P. MCLAINE, Director, Eastern European Division, Department of External Affairs: 1 April 1982

MICHAEL MILROY, Vice-President and General Manager, Canadian Association – Latin America and the Caribbean: 18 March 1982

TAD MITSUI, Associate Secretary for World Concerns, Canadian Council of Churches: 9 March 1982

JOHN MORGAN, President, Canadian Peace Congress: 18 March 1982

M. NIXON, Program Officer, Refugee Policy Division, Recruitment and Selection Branch, Department of Employment and Immigration: 1 April 1982

BEA OLIVASTRI, Executive Director, National Survival Institute: 18 May 1982

JOHN O'MANIQUE, School of International Affairs, Carleton University: 1 April 1982

D.M. PAGE, Deputy Director, Historical Division, Department of External Affairs: 7 April 1982

LUCIE PÉPIN, President, Canadian Advisory Council on the Status of Women: 31 March 1982

LEWIS PERINBAM, Vice-President, Special Programs Branch, CIDA: 6 April 1982

H.R. PINAULT, Managing Director, Association of Consulting Engineers of Canada: 26 May 1982

RENATE PRATT, Co-ordinator, Taskforce on Churches and Corporate Responsibility: 20 April 1982

DAVID PROTHEROE, CIDA: 29 March 1982

RUTH RAYMOND, Canadian Jewish Congress: 11 March 1982

ROSS F. REID, Executive Director, Consulting Engineers of Ontario: 5 May 1982

DAVID ROBIN, Research and Information Officer, Consumers' Association of Canada: 20 May 1982

ROGER ROLF, Regional Education Officer, Oxfam Canada: 19 May 1982

E.F. ROOTS, Executive Secretary, Canadian Environmental Advisory Council, Department of the Environment: 6 April 1982

PETER SCHIBLER, President, Swiss Canadian Chamber of Commerce (Montreal) Inc: 26 May 1982

LARRY SOLOMAN, Research Associate, Energy Probe: 11 March 1982

J. STARK, Director, Operation Dismantle: 2 April 1982

RYLA SNYDER, Librarian, Canadian Federation of Independent Business: 18 March 1982

W. SZCZESNY, First Vice-President, Association of United Ukrainian Canadians: 18 May 1982

L. THIBAULT, Executive Vice-President, Canadian Manufacturers' Association: 9 March 1982

S. UYEYAMA, Arms Control and Disarmament Division, Department of External Affairs: 31 March 1982

M.S. VARDY, Export Manager and Manager of Industrial Trades, Canadian Manufacturers' Association: 7 April 1982

JAMES A. WELLER, General Manager, Canadian Nuclear Association: 9 March 1982

DANIELLE WETHERUP, Acting Director, International Programs Branch, Department of the Environment: 5 April 1982

REDE WIDSTRAND, Resource Centre, School of International Affairs, Carleton University: 29 March 1982

JOHN WILLIS, Representative, Greenpeace: 8 March 1982

NANCI WOODS, Public Affairs Assistant, Canadian Petroleum Association: 26 May 1982

R.T.Y. YANG, Director, International Policy (Air), Transport Canada: 6 April 1982

ROGER YOUNG, North-South Institute: 31 March 1982

ERIC ZINMAN, Representative, Operation Dismantle: 26 May 1982

INDEX TO ORGANIZATIONS